# HOPE

## FOR A GLOBAL ETHIC

# HOPE

## FOR A GLOBAL ETHIC

SHARED PRINCIPLES IN RELIGIOUS SCRIPTURES

by

**Brian D. Lepard**

*Bahá'í*
PUBLISHING
**Wilmette, Illinois**

Bahá'í Publishing, 415 Linden Avenue, Wilmette, IL 60091-2844
Copyright © by the National Spiritual Assembly
of the Bahá'ís of the United States
All Rights Reserved. Published 2005
Printed in the United States of America on acid-free paper ∞

08  07  06  05     1   2   3   4

Library of Congress Cataloging-in-Publication Data
Lepard, Brian D.
    Hope for a global ethic : shared principles in religious scriptures / Brian
D. Lepard.
        p. cm.
    Includes bibliographical references.
    ISBN 1-931847-20-7
    1. Bahai ethics. 2. Religious ethics—Comparative studies. 3. Sacred
    books.  I. Title.

BJ1288.L47 2005
205—dc22
                                                    2005050727

Cover design by Robert A. Reddy
Book design by Suni D. Hannan

# CONTENTS

*To my children*

# Acknowledgments

This book could not have been written without the expert guidance of many scholars and colleagues who selflessly contributed their time and advice to the project. I am particularly grateful to the many religion and philosophy scholars who reviewed relevant portions of various drafts of the book. These include Arvind Sharma of McGill University and Robert N. Minor of the University of Kansas (Hinduism); Michael J. Broyde of Emory Law School and Lenn Goodman of Vanderbilt University (Judaism); Taitetsu Unno, Emeritus, of Smith College and Dale Wright of Occidental College (Buddhism); Irene Bloom, Emerita, of Barnard College's Department of Asian and Middle Eastern Cultures and E. Bruce Brooks of the Warring States Project at the University of Massachusetts at Amherst (Confucianism); John Langan, S.J. of Georgetown University and Sidnie W. Crawford of the University of Nebraska (Christianity); Khaled Abou El Fadl of the UCLA School of Law, Abdullahi Ahmed An-Na'im of the Emory Law School, Syed Nomanul Haq of the University of Pennsylvania, Ann Elizabeth Mayer of the Wharton School of the University of Pennsylvania, and Abdulaziz Sachedina of the University of Virginia (Islam); and Firuz Kazemzadeh, Emeritus, of Yale University (the Bahá'í Faith). I also greatly appreciate the suggestions of Robert Audi and the late Philip Quinn, both of the University of Notre Dame.

Furthermore, I benefited from the encouragement and comments of various scholars who participated in conferences held at Chapman University in April 1999 on human rights and responsibilities in the world religions, and in March 2000 on ethics and world religions. I am especially indebted to Arvind Sharma, Nancy Martin of Chapman University, and Joseph Runzo of Chapman University, who organized the conferences and encouraged me to participate.

I warmly thank a number of personal friends who reviewed portions of the manuscript and offered their advice, including Isabella Bunn, Julie Carpenter, Neda Molai, Tanvir Shah, Thomas Ukinski, and Michael Weisser. And I benefited from the comments and encouragement of many colleagues at the University of Nebraska College of Law, including former Dean Nancy Rapoport and current Dean Steven Willborn. Completion of this project would never have been possible without the moral and financial support of the University of Nebraska College of Law. I especially appreciated research grants provided by the Ross McCollum Law College Fund and offered by Dean Nancy Rapoport and Dean Willborn. Further, the library staff of the Law College provided indispensable assistance with my research. I wish to thank Kris Lauber in particular for her help over the many years required for the completion of this book, which she always offered with cheerfulness no matter how great the demands placed on her. And my former secretary Marcy Tintera kindly assisted in the preparation of the manuscript.

I am grateful for the guidance of Terry Cassiday and Christopher Martin of Bahá'í Publishing. Their suggestions greatly improved the manuscript and made it much more readable. And I could not wish for a more meticulous and thoughtful editor than Christopher Martin.

Finally, I express my heartfelt gratitude to my family. My parents helped instill in me a deep appreciation for the unity of religions based on the teachings of the Bahá'í Faith. And my wife Jenina and sons Greg and Brandon have provided constant love and encouragement. I am eternally indebted to them. My children in particular, and their keen understanding of the ethical principles common to the scriptures of the world religions, provide the clearest evidence that hope for a global ethic is indeed well-founded.

# Note on the Transliteration of Foreign Words and Names

In this work I have transliterated foreign words and proper names. As a general rule, but with some exceptions, I have used diacriticals for words and names in Arabic, Pali, and Sanskrit. Regarding romanization of Chinese terms, all forms quoted from Brooks and Brooks, *The Original Analects*, are in Common Alphabetic. Otherwise, I have used the Pinyin form. With a few exceptions, I have generally employed the Cambridge system of transliteration of Arabic when discussing Islam and its sacred texts. I have used a modified form of the Cambridge system typically found in the Bahá'í writings when discussing the Bahá'í Faith and its scriptures.

# Preface

This book had its beginnings in another project—a book about the legal issues involved in the use of military force to protect desperate victims of human rights violations. In the process of undertaking research for that book, I perceived that the legal problems of so-called "humanitarian intervention" were closely interrelated with important ethical issues. And it seemed to me that the world religions were potent sources of ethical inspiration for most people and governments around the world. This conviction was inspired in large part by my beliefs as a member of the Bahá'í Faith. As a Bahá'í, I had long believed in the common divine origin and essential unity of the world's major religions. But I had not undertaken a systematic review of the revered scriptures of the world. I therefore began researching the sacred scriptures of the seven religions with the most geographically dispersed global membership, including the Bahá'í Faith.

I discovered, in the course of my investigations, that many common ethical principles in fact could be mined from the scriptures of the world religions. Further, these shared principles supported similar principles in contemporary international law. Accordingly, I developed in my book, titled *Rethinking Humanitarian Intervention,* an argument that decisions about humanitarian intervention should be made based on fundamental ethical principles common to international law and world religions. In particular, they should be made in light of principles related to a preeminent principle of "unity in diversity."

This book focuses on the commonalities I found in the ethical teachings of the scriptures of the world religions, and it develops the preliminary evidence for a "global ethic" first presented in *Rethinking Humanitarian Intervention*. I hope it will encourage all of us to begin a conversation with one another, and with our leaders, on how these fundamental ethical principles can be put into practice to meet the urgent needs of a troubled global community.

# 1

## Is There Hope for a Global Ethic?

# Is There Hope for
# a Global Ethic?

"How could this happen?" This depressing question has preoccupied many of us after the atrocities of September 11, 2001. The general answer provided by the investigation that followed—that the attacks were committed by fanatical devotees of Islam who viewed it as their religious duty to kill Americans—has in turn raised another burning question: "Can there possibly be any hope for a global ethic, particularly in a world that is traumatized by terrorism, war, gross human rights violations, and religious division and hatred?"

There are three principal reasons for us to come to the pessimistic conclusion, "not in the near future." First, there is no end to the social ills that plague the world community at the dawn of the twenty-first century, leading many people to feel a profound sense of despair. Second, these ailments raise scores of troubling questions that would need to be addressed by a global ethic. And third, the rift between some Islamic and Western world views revealed by the attacks of September 11 seems to exemplify a deeper, broader disagreement among the peoples of the world about how to solve global problems. This disagreement appears today to create a forbidding obstacle to reaching accord on a worldwide moral standard.

# Problems Facing the
# World Community

The attacks of September 11, 2001, forever punctured in the minds of Americans any illusions that we are safe from the destructive gales of fanaticism and terrorism so depressingly familiar to residents of the Middle East and other troubled areas of the globe. Numerous wars, including in Iraq, but particularly in underdeveloped areas of the world, such as Africa, claim countless lives annually and leave many other victims horribly injured and disabled.[1] The Middle East continues to be a hotbed of ethnic and religious strife. Many of these terrorist attacks, wars, and conflicts have been fueled by religious fanaticism and prejudice.

At the same time, and often as a direct result of wars and civil conflicts, millions of individuals around the world endure violations of their fundamental human rights. They suffer from starvation and a lack of sufficient clothing, shelter, and medical care; are arrested and imprisoned, tortured, or executed without a fair trial or even a trial at all; are raped; are discriminated against or persecuted by reason of their race, ethnicity, nationality, gender, or religion; are silenced if they hold unpopular views; and are denied their right to practice freely their own religion.

In the economic realm, the materialistic culture pervading the West has, with the fall of Communism, been able to gain a foothold in other parts of the world. It has spawned increasing demands by residents of developing countries for consumer goods and a higher standard of living. These demands have propelled the process of economic "globalization," leading to greater economic wealth for many businesses able to take advantage of these demands. Meanwhile, despite globalization and the enhancement of international trade, an unconscionable number of individuals in much of the developing world continue to suffer from debilitating poverty.[2]

The enhanced economic power of the West has encouraged the view of many non-Western political leaders that the West seeks cultural hegemony. These leaders have played on the fears of members of the global population who are dejected that their anticipated economic expectations have not been realized. They have exploited age-old prejudices to scapegoat "others" from a different ethnic, racial, or religious group. These leaders and others have made bold assertions of cultural identity that reject any possibility of reconciliation with other cultures or of the evolution of a world culture, including a universal ethic. Instead, they have advanced the notion of "cultural relativism"—that there are no true global ethical norms. The proponents of relativism argue that ethics is inextricably tied to particular cultures and that cultures are necessarily diverse and at some level irreconcilable. These trends and views have led political scientist Samuel P. Huntington to declare that future conflicts will be driven by a "clash of civilizations," and as we watch the daily news, we may find it easy to sympathize with this perspective.[3]

These divisive forces, however, appear simultaneously to be counteracted by a variety of harmonizing forces—of trends toward greater unity and cooperation among the diverse peoples of the world. For example, through the United Nations, states have attempted to intervene both diplomatically and militarily to prevent, or at least contain, many of the conflicts that have erupted in recent years. The public may generally regard these attempts as failures. But these interventions have shown a nascent will on the part of many governments to work cooperatively to restore peace and achieve some minimal level of enjoyment of human rights. The UN has adopted numerous treaties and declarations specifying human rights, including the 1948 Universal Declaration of Human Rights. In the early 1990s, the United Nations established ad hoc war crime tribunals for the former Yugoslavia and Rwanda, and many of its member states established a permanent international criminal court in July 2002. And in the economic sphere, world trade talks, while contentious, have at least begun to address concerns about unreasonable barriers to international trade and the enhancement of economic growth worldwide. They have also tried to remedy undesirable attendant problems, such as the exploitation of workers and the uneven distribution of economic wealth.

If these unifying forces are ultimately to hold sway over the destructive ones and keep them in check, they must be motivated by more than a simple desire to correct social ills. They must be anchored in, and fortified by, a veritable global ethic. Only a global ethic—a relatively specific set of shared ethical principles—will ultimately be sufficient to support these more positive trends.

# Some Crucial Issues That Need to be Addressed by a Global Ethic

As the above brief survey makes clear, a global ethic must address a number of crucial ethical issues that today are the focus of much debate. For example, many claims are being made that our primary allegiance, morally, ought to be to our own ethnic or religious group, or to our own country. In the United States we are taught the virtues of patriotism, especially after the attacks of September 11, 2001. But are these moral claims legitimate? Or, for example, should we instead morally consider ourselves as members of one human family first, and Americans only second?

Other important ethical issues involve the personal virtues we ought to cultivate and the moral duties to others we ought to recognize. For example, should we primarily value our own individual autonomy and the pursuit of our economic wealth, or should we renounce the pursuit of our own self-interest and instead show generosity to others? Do we all have a moral obligation to treat others as we would wish ourselves to be treated—that is, to follow the "Golden Rule"—or only a minimal obligation not to harm others or interfere with their own exercise of freedom? And what obligations do we have to provide assistance to the injured, the sick, the destitute, or those who are oppressed by governments or their fellow citizens?

Advocates of cultural, racial, or religious separatism often argue for the inherent superiority of their own group. Are these claims justified? Or should all of us as human beings be considered to have an equal spiritual and social dignity? Do we all have certain inviolable human "rights" that we can claim, or should we instead hope for charitable and beneficent treatment from others, which is certainly commendable, but is not our "right"? Do we have a right to life and to physical security? Do we have a similar right to the bare necessities of food, clothing, and shelter necessary to keep us alive and healthy? Or is the enjoyment of these necessities merely a desirable social goal, rather than our right? What rights should women enjoy? What rights should members of minorities enjoy?

Similarly, we can ask: What rights do individuals and religious communities have to freely practice their own religion without fear of oppression by a government or by members of other religious groups? Religious scriptures have often been used by believers to justify religious warfare or terrorism, as in the case of the September 11 terrorists. But are these uses of scripture warranted or ethically justifiable?

Human rights issues raise another set of questions about the role of governments. What is the function of government—to promote the interests of the governors, the cohesion of society, minimal social order, or the well-being of the individual members of the governed society? Are nation-states entitled to a high degree of autonomy or "sovereignty"? Some Americans are arguing against US participation in international organizations and human rights treaties based on a claimed infringement of US sovereignty. Is the sovereignty of states ethically limited, especially by obligations to protect human rights?

Another set of questions we face revolves around a practical problem: How should we resolve ethical and political difficulties? Through the use of force? Through law, including international criminal law? Through bargaining between states, groups, or individuals, with the hope of reaching a compromise that will at least partially satisfy everyone, further their self-interests, and avoid open conflict? Through a system of decision making by simple majority vote? Or through a process of consultation in which we approach the problem with open minds and a willingness to consider the merits of the views advanced by others, perhaps followed by a vote?

The resurgence in the aftermath of the Cold War of separatist wars and claims by various groups to a right to secede highlights many perplexing problems. For example, when, if ever, do groups like Kosovo Albanians or Iraqi rebels have a right to disobey the law or an established government and take up arms in opposition? And what obligations do all of us have to respect our government and obey the law?

These issues raise another question: Is peace, by itself, always a value that ought to be promoted? Should it always take precedence over justice? If not, when can concerns about justice override the maintenance of peace? The raging conflict in the Middle East shows how difficult it is for aggrieved groups like Israelis or Palestinians to make peace when they feel that they are the victims of grave injustices. And how, in any case, should we define peace? Is it the absence of overt violence, or is it a state of affairs that also incorporates some degree of justice and respect for human rights?

In the sphere of international relations, large and small states alike have often disregarded, or even openly defied, their treaty obligations. For example, many observers believe that in 2003 the US violated the UN Charter when it launched a war against Iraq without the explicit approval of the United Nations Security Council. Others, however, defend the Iraq war as consistent with the charter.[4] This action and others by many states raise ethical questions to ponder. For example, what level of respect ought to be given to treaty obligations? Is there a moral obligation to honor treaties, or should states feel free to disregard treaties when they conflict with other state policy goals, such as maintaining security? More generally, is there an ethical obligation to promote the development of international law and cooperation among nations? Or are states ethically entitled to focus on promoting their own interests? In recent discussions in the US on the war against terrorism we see evidence of widely divergent views on these questions.

Indeed, the wars raging in the world raise many challenging ethical problems. When, if ever, is the use of force justified, and for what purposes? Is there some moral obligation to undertake otherwise legitimate military action in collaboration with other states where possible? And what limitations on how war is pursued should be observed to help protect civilians from death or injury? Is it permissible to bomb populated areas if there is no other way to undertake a legitimate military objective, such as putting an end to massacres, disabling terrorist groups, or eliminating weapons of mass destruction? Or are there more absolute moral restraints on the conduct of hostilities that apply to all warfare regardless of the justness of the underlying cause?

During the last decade and a half the international community has made a number of attempts to use military force to prevent or thwart gross violations of human rights. These have included military action in such troubled lands as Somalia, Bosnia, Rwanda, Haiti, Kosovo, East Timor, the Democratic Republic of the Congo, Afghanistan, Iraq, and the Sudan. Many observers have defended the Iraq war as a legitimate humanitarian intervention, but others have disagreed. Is military intervention for humanitarian purposes morally justified? Is it ever morally required? If so, when?

Finally, the horrible humanitarian crises that have shaken human society in recent decades, and indeed the last century, have cast a dark cloud over hopes that human beings and their leaders can ever be persuaded to reform their conduct in an ethical way. Rather, they understandably can make us skeptical and even cause us to despair. But is this kind of attitude ethically appropriate? Are there ethical grounds for us to feel optimistic? And is there room for a middle ground between pessimism and optimism that would allow us both to acknowledge current problems and to attempt to address them as best we can, even if we cannot solve all of them at once?

# Obstacles to a Global Ethic

There are no straightforward answers to the above questions. This would be true even if all inhabitants of the planet adhered to the same religion or philosophy. Achieving any kind of agreement on a resolution is even more challenging in a world characterized by religious and philosophical diversity. Indeed, the clamor of diverse and often clashing religious perspectives at first suggests that agreement on a common core of fundamental ethical principles that can answer the above questions is not only unlikely, but for all intents and purposes, impossible.

Numerous scholars have concluded that the prospects for a global ethic are slim indeed. For example, law professor Thomas Franck has argued that "as for the world, while it may be taking shape as a secular political community, it has barely begun to coalesce into a moral community with universally shared or overlapping values and concepts of justice, and is unlikely to do so in the foreseeable future. . . . Iranian Shiite fundamentalists, Irish Catholics, Orthodox Israelis, Indian Hindu secularists, American Episcopalians, and West

African Animists may share a world of states and secular rules, but not a common system of values, a globalized understanding of fairness, or a shared canon of justice principles."[5]

This kind of skepticism is understandable. Clearly there are many fundamental differences in values among the world's peoples, including adherents to different religions. Further, the intensity of religiously motivated nationalism, separatism, and terrorism throughout the globe naturally creates significant doubt that the world religions can ever serve as the basis for restoring civil peace and respecting human rights, let alone provide the foundation for agreement on a global ethic.[6] But are these obstacles to the evolution of a global ethic insurmountable? Or is there some possibility that agreement might be reached on a system of ethical principles that can begin to suggest answers to contemporary ethical dilemmas?

# The Role of Scriptures in Fostering a Global Ethic

I suggest that there is indeed a possibility for the development of a global ethic—and that the scriptures of the various religions that are so often viewed as the source of ethical disagreement and discord may provide the foundation for such an ethic. Indeed, I propose that religious scriptures have a unique potential to do so because they manifest many ethical convergences, on which I will elaborate in the following chapters. Additionally, the scriptures of world religions play a major role in shaping how people view fundamental moral concepts such as right and wrong. Religion scholars Ninian Smart and Richard D. Hecht have noted that the "world's sacred texts are potent sources of inspiration and behaviour and, more importantly, they play a crucial part in the formation of peoples' perception of reality. . . . The scriptures of a particular community are normative for its worship, for doctrine and for behaviour."[7]

This book draws upon selected scriptures of the seven world religions with the most broadly dispersed global membership according to a widely cited survey. These are Christianity (238 countries), the Bahá'í Faith (218 countries), Islam (206 countries), Judaism (134 countries), Buddhism (129 countries), Hinduism (114 countries), and Confucianism and "Chinese Universism" (91 countries). These religions rank among the eight largest in total worldwide membership, and their members constitute about 79 percent of the total world population.[8]

I hope to demonstrate that selected passages from the scriptures of these world religions may be interpreted to endorse certain common ethical principles. My concern is not with intricate theological problems but with enduring and general norms of social morality. Further, the short discussion in this book, which intentionally has been kept to a manageable length, represents only a tiny glimpse of a vast primary and secondary literature from each religious system. There are many excellent books that provide a far more detailed and thorough analysis of each religion and its scriptures. I have provided references to some of these works in the bibliography so that interested readers can pursue further research.

# Selected Scriptures from Seven World Religions

In this book I discuss the seven religions mentioned above and their scriptures in the approximate chronological sequence of the genesis of each religious belief system. I have chosen to study, for most religions, only a small number of central scriptures and in many instances only one. I will now discuss these scriptures and provide some brief background information on each religion.

First, Hinduism is one of the most ancient religions, extending back approximately four thousand years, with its earliest textual sources, the Vedas, dating from about 1400 BCE. It is the most prominent religion in India. Central to Hinduism during the period of the philosophical works known as the Upanishads (about 700–500 BCE), considered to be the last part of the Vedic corpus, is the concept of *dharma*. Dharma means both the binding law of the sacred Hindu texts and an expression of eternal, "natural law." The Bhagavad Gita, a work of poetry that contains the teachings of the prophet Krishna and was most likely composed in the third or fourth century BCE, is part of the great post-Vedic epic known as the *Mahabharata*. It expounds upon the requirements of a devotional life as well as the obligations of dharma. One scholar has noted that in contemporary times it has won acceptance "as the primary scripture of Hinduism."[9] For these reasons, I will focus here on the Bhagavad Gita.

According to the Bhagavad Gita, Krishna was a manifestation of God in human form, but he was not the only one. Krishna said, "I come into being in age after age."[10] The Gita is structured as a dialogue between Krishna and Arjuna, a member of the warrior caste, who is hesitating to fight an opposing army that includes his relatives. In the course of this dialogue, Krishna explains the principles of a spiritual life.

Moses, the most revered prophet in Judaism, instructed the people of Israel in the period around 1250 BCE. The Hebrew scriptures, upon which I focus here, consist of the five Books of Moses (the Pentateuch or Torah), the books of the prophets (Nevi'im), and the writings (Kethuvim). Moses claimed to be a Prophet of God—"I make known the laws and teachings of God"—and the Torah has a corresponding special authority for Jews as God's revealed word. Jews also turn for guidance to the writings and books of the later Jewish prophets and to subsequent writings of rabbis.[11]

Buddhism's diverse denominations all revere the person known as Gautama, the Buddha ("the Enlightened One"), who traditionally is thought to have been born in Nepal in about 563 BCE. Buddhist literature is voluminous, and there is no single authoritative text akin to the Torah in Judaism or the Koran in Islam. Indeed, because Buddhist scriptures were recorded long after the Buddha's death, it is particularly difficult to verify the authenticity of words attributed to him. Moreover, many of contemporary Buddhism's schools, such as Mahayana Buddhism, have their own revered texts. Nevertheless, there is a core of scriptures generally regarded by all schools as authoritative, and it is upon these that I will primarily draw.[12]

The historical Buddha did not claim to be a prophet or manifestation of a divine entity. According to later texts, he indicated that he was but one of many Buddhas who had already appeared throughout history and would come again under the name Maitreya. Indeed, in Buddhist scriptures the title of "the Buddha" refers to "a man who has first enlightened himself and will thereafter enlighten others." According to Buddhist literature, the historical Buddha was born a prince but went on to lead a life of spiritual contemplation and endeavor, first submitting himself to fasting and austerity, and then preaching the virtues of the "middle way" and becoming a profound teacher. Although the Buddha exemplified a life of humility, he maintained that he was unique in needing no teacher of his own to achieve *nirvana*. Nirvana is the highest spiritual state in which one is freed from the material cycle of birth and death: "Nirvana have I now obtained, and I am not the same as others are. Quite by myself, you see, have I the Dharma won. . . . That is the reason why I am a Buddha."[13] It is because of this special station that the Buddha is so highly venerated among Buddhists.

The great thinker known as Confucius in the West, born around 551 BCE, taught, together with his successors, many principles and rules of ethical conduct. Confucian thought has exercised an important influence in China over many centuries. Many of Confucius's reputed sayings are collected and recorded in the Analects, which is believed by some contemporary scholars such as E. Bruce Brooks and A. Taeko Brooks ("Brooks and Brooks") to include original sayings of Confucius himself as well as later accretions written over the course of some 230 years by various successors. One modern Confucian scholar has referred to the Analects as "the most revered sacred scripture in the Confucian tradition."[14] I focus on the Analects because it is the central book of Confucianism. However, I also pay attention to the works of another influential Confucian teacher, Mencius (circa 372–289 BCE), who lived a couple of centuries after Confucius. Mencius's book of works is, along with the Analects, one of the four major books of Confucianism.

The ethical teachings of Jesus, who was born in about 4 BCE, are recorded in the books of the New Testament. Many Christians believe, according to the New Testament, that Jesus is the Son of God as well as God in human form. Their belief is based on Jesus's assertions, among others, that "The Father and I are one" and that "Whoever has seen me has seen the Father." The New Testament consists of 27 books, whose authority was generally accepted by most Christians by the fourth century of the Christian era. The books of the New Testament include the Gospels, which are "works about the acts and teachings of Jesus," Acts, which documents "early missionary activity," and letters or epistles, including letters of St. Paul. The New Testament also includes the Book of Revelation.

One scholar notes that "all Christian groups, no matter how they may be divided on other theological issues, acknowledge the authority of the New Testament."[15] In the New Testament, Jesus reaffirmed many of the ethical teachings in the Hebrew scriptures, but also taught new ethical principles. Thus, Christians also revere the Hebrew scriptures.

For Muslims, the Koran is the word of God as it was revealed to the prophet Muḥammad (570–632 CE) and therefore has divine authority. It is Islam's most holy and revered text. Muḥammad claimed to be a Messenger of God, following earlier Messengers such as Moses and Jesus and continuing the outpouring of divine revelation through them. But he did not claim to be God: "I am only a mortal, like you are. To me it has been revealed that your God is One God." Classical Islamic jurisprudence recognizes a number of additional sources of authority. Alongside the Koran, Muslims look for guidance to authoritative *hadiths*, or traditions, which are sayings or practices of Muḥammad collected during the early centuries of Islam.[16] My discussion of ethical principles will generally concentrate on the Koran itself. However, I will make reference where appropriate to hadiths and to the opinions of Islamic scholars and jurists.

Finally, the Bahá'í Faith is the youngest of the world religions surveyed in this book.[17] It reveres two "Manifestations" of God. The first is the Báb (the "Gate") (1819–50), who founded the Bábí religion in Persia (now Iran) in 1844, and who foretold the coming of a greater Manifestation to follow him. The second is Bahá'u'lláh (the "Glory of God") (1817–92), who in 1863 declared that he was the one promised by the Báb. Bahá'u'lláh's followers became known as Bahá'ís and his religion as the Bahá'í Faith.

Bahá'u'lláh affirmed that the founders of all the major religions—including Noah, Abraham, Moses, Jesus, and Muḥammad—were divinely inspired Manifestations of one God who provided eternal spiritual guidance to humankind and social teachings that varied with the needs of the age in which each appeared. He proclaimed that he was the latest, but not the last, of these Manifestations.[18] Bahá'u'lláh wrote many volumes in his own pen and clearly designated his son 'Abdu'l-Bahá (1844–1921) as the authorized interpreter of his teachings. 'Abdu'l-Bahá in turn appointed his grandson Shoghi Effendi (1897–1957) as Guardian of the Bahá'í Faith, with authority to interpret his writings and those of Bahá'u'lláh. Six years after Shoghi Effendi's death in 1957, the world Bahá'í community elected, as foreseen in Bahá'u'lláh's writings, the first international governing body of the Bahá'í Faith, known as the Universal House of Justice. In this book I concentrate on the writings of Bahá'u'lláh, 'Abdu'l-Bahá, and Shoghi Effendi. However, the Bahá'í teachings regard only the writings of Bahá'u'lláh, the Báb, and 'Abdu'l-Bahá as sacred scripture.

# A Word About the Challenges of Scriptural Interpretation

Scriptural interpretation is a notoriously contentious subject—so contentious, indeed, that many of us are apt to believe that, like a Rorschach blot, we can find whatever we want in any scripture. While there is no doubt that at one level there are as many interpretive approaches as there are interpreters, a number of interpretive methods have won a wide following. These include a literal, textual method, based on the supposed "plain meaning" of words; a method that attempts to ascertain the author's intentions; an approach that recognizes that many passages may be allegorical or symbolic; a

sociohistorical approach that attempts to interpret scriptures in light
of the social and historical conditions existing at the time they were
written, and that accepts the revision of an original meaning in
order to adapt it to current social realities; and a thematic approach
that attempts to understand a particular passage in the context of
other passages in the scripture and to ascertain how it relates to
certain broad themes developed throughout the scripture.

I could not presume to develop in this short book a sophisticated
approach to scriptural interpretation. Rather, I simply acknowledge the potential validity of the above approaches and draw on
many of them in suggesting that certain interpretations are possible. And I do accept, and implicitly adopt, a view of scripture
developed in the Bahá'í writings. The Bahá'í writings indicate that
all religions have taught the same eternal spiritual principles but
have varied in their social legislation, which has evolved over time
to meet the needs of the particular age in which each religion was
revealed. For example, 'Abdu'l-Bahá stated,

> The Law of God is divided into two parts. One is the fundamen-
> tal basis which comprises all spiritual things—that is to say, it
> refers to the spiritual virtues and divine qualities; this does not
> change nor alter: it is the Holy of Holies, which is the essence of
> the Law of Adam, Noah, Abraham, Moses, Christ, Muḥammad,
> the Báb and Bahá'u'lláh, and which lasts and is established in all
> the prophetic cycles. It will never be abrogated, for it is spiritual
> and not material truth; it is faith, knowledge, certitude, justice,
> piety, righteousness, trustworthiness, love of God, benevolence,
> purity, detachment, humility, meekness, patience and constancy.
> It shows mercy to the poor, defends the oppressed, gives to the
> wretched and uplifts the fallen. . . .
>
> The second part of the Religion of God, which refers to the
> material world, and which comprises fasting, prayer, forms of

worship, marriage and divorce, the abolition of slavery, legal pro-cesses, transactions, indemnities for murder, violence, theft and injuries—this part of the Law of God, which refers to material things, is modified and altered in each prophetic cycle in accordance with the necessities of the times.[19]

In keeping with this perspective, my focus is on the identification of general and timeless ethical principles, not on the particular social legislation of each religion. Nevertheless, I mention certain aspects of social legislation because specific social laws may provide evidence about the universal principles underlying them.

# 2

# Unity in Diversity

*In a knowledge-and-cultivation-perfected / Brahman, a cow, an elephant, / And in a mere dog, and an outcaste, / The wise see the same thing.*

—Krishna

# The Unity of the Human Family

The world's scriptures express a fundamental conviction that all of us as human beings should be united as members of one family. For example, the Bhagavad Gita calls for a spiritual unity among all human beings through moral discipline: "Disciplined in discipline, with purified self, / Self-subdued, with senses overcome, / His self become (one with) the self of all beings." In another place the Bhagavad Gita refers to the "whole world" being "united." One Hindu scholar has asserted that an essential Hindu teaching is that the "whole human family is one and basically indivisible."[1]

The Torah affirms that we should love our neighbors as ourselves. And the Hebrew scriptures ask rhetorically, with an implied affirmative answer: "Have we not all one Father? Did not one God create us?" Further, there are two covenants: one between God and Moses and the Israelites and the other between God and Noah and his descendants. The latter "Noachide" covenant applies to all of us.[2]

According to Buddhist scriptures, the Buddha stated, "It is for the weal of the world that a Buddha has won enlightenment, and the welfare of all that lives has been his aim." And Buddhist scriptures urge us to care for others with the same loving concern that a mother would express for her child: "Even as a mother watches over and protects her child, her only child, so with a boundless mind should one cherish all living beings, radiating friendliness

23

over the entire world, above, below, and all around without limit. So let him cultivate a boundless good will towards the entire world, uncramped, free from ill-will or enmity." The Buddha further taught that mankind belongs to one biological species.[3]

The teachings of the Analects encourage us to see each other as brothers. In particular, one of Confucius's followers said to another, "If a gentleman [a virtuous person, whether male or female] is assiduous and omits nothing, is respectful to others and displays decorum, then within the Four Seas, all are his brothers. Why should a gentleman worry that he has no brothers?"[4]

Jesus renewed the Torah's commandment to love our neighbors as ourselves. In the story of the Good Samaritan, Jesus explained who a "neighbor" is for the purpose of this commandment. In the story, a Samaritan came upon a man who had been assaulted by robbers. While others passed by, the Good Samaritan stopped and cared for the man, dressing his wounds and bringing him to an inn. According to Jesus, the person who showed mercy for the beaten man, the Good Samaritan, was a "neighbor" to the man. Jesus thus articulated a conception of "neighbor" based not on our geographical proximity to one another, but on our capacity to care for any one of our fellow members of the human family. It is noteworthy, too, that the Samaritan would have been regarded as a religious heretic. This aspect of the story emphasizes, therefore, the unity and "neighborliness" of people from different and even antagonistic religious faiths.[5]

St. Paul underscored this central aspect of the Christian religion: "There is no distinction between Jew and Greek; the same Lord is Lord of all and is generous to all who call on him." And in Galatians, he stated similarly, "There is no longer Jew or Greek, there is no longer slave or free, there is no longer male and female; for all of you are one in Christ Jesus." Citizenship is ultimately divine and universal: "Our citizenship is in heaven." St. Paul affirmed that Jesus's teachings united Gentiles and Jews: "In his flesh he has made both groups into one and has broken down the dividing wall, that is, the hostility between us. He has abolished the law with its commandments and ordinances, that he might create in himself one new humanity in place of the two, thus making peace. . . . So then you are no longer strangers and aliens, but you are citizens with the saints and also members of the household of God."[6]

According to the Koran, all of us were fashioned by God from one soul: "Mankind, fear your Lord, who created you of a single soul." The Koran also affirms that we are all children of Adam: "We have honoured the Children of Adam and carried them on land and sea, and provided them with good things, and preferred them greatly over many of those We created." The Koran, moreover, asserts that God originally established the entire human family as one community: "The people were one nation; then God sent forth the Prophets, good tidings to bear and warning, and He sent down with them the Book with the truth, that He might decide between the people touching their differences." Likewise it emphasizes, "Mankind were only one nation, then they fell into variance." And again it states, "'Surely this community of yours is one community, and I am your Lord; so serve Me.'" One hadith says that the "whole universe is the family of Allah."[7]

The pivotal teaching of Bahá'u'lláh is the fundamental unity of humankind. Bahá'u'lláh announced, "It is not for him to pride himself who loveth his own country, but rather for him who loveth the whole world. The earth is but one country, and mankind its citizens." Bahá'u'lláh further proclaimed, "The well-being of mankind, its peace and security, are unattainable unless and until its unity is firmly established." In the words of Shoghi Effendi, "Unification of the whole of mankind is the hall-mark of the stage which human society is now approaching. Unity of family, of tribe, of city-state, and nation have been successively attempted and fully established. World unity is the goal towards which a harassed humanity is striving."[8]

# The Positive Value of Diversity within the Context of the Unity of the Human Family

Passages from almost all the scriptures recognize the legitimacy of religious communities, nations, and other groups within the global human community. They implicitly endorse our right as individuals to take pride in these associations, and they assure us of the value of unity and agreement among members of these communities. But many passages, including those just quoted, simultaneously suggest that a concern for the entire human family is morally superior to any lesser communal sentiments we may feel. Taken together, these various passages imply that we are moral participants in expanding circles of community and cooperation that ultimately extend to the whole of the human race. The scriptures therefore value both the spiritual unity of the human race *and* diversity, and they do not see the two as incompatible. In short, they uphold a principle of "unity in diversity."

For example, the Bhagavad Gita validates the existence of castes and gives caste ties ethical legitimacy. But it also suggests that one's caste identity is morally unimportant. For example, it affirms, "In a knowledge-and-cultivation-perfected / Brahman, a cow, an elephant, / And in a mere dog, and an outcaste, / The wise see the same thing." Religion scholar Franklin Edgerton has suggested that this verse manifests a high standard of ethics similar to the biblical injunction that "Thou shalt love thy neighbor as thyself."[9]

In the case of the Hebrew scriptures, although God's covenant with Moses appears to grant Jews a privileged rank among other peoples, it also imposes greater obligations on Jews. In the Hebrew scriptures God often chastised and punished the Jews for ignoring these obligations. For example, Ezekiel states, "Thus said the Lord God: I set this Jerusalem in the midst of nations, with countries round about her. But she rebelled against My rules and My laws, acting more wickedly than the nations and the countries round about her." The book of Isaiah treats Israel as one nation among many, including its historical enemies, and affirms that they and their people are all equally blessed in the sight of God: "Israel shall be a third partner with Egypt and Assyria as a blessing on earth; for the Lord of Hosts will bless them, saying, 'Blessed be My people Egypt, My handiwork Assyria, and My very own Israel.'"[10]

Thus, the Hebrew scriptures, and especially the books of the later prophets, exhibit a humanity-oriented outlook alongside the Torah's apparent emphasis on Jewish nationhood. Historian Norman Bentwich notes in this connection that while in "the historical books of the Bible, the God of Israel is a jealous national God, reigning alone and requiring a higher ethical conduct of his people than any other religion of antiquity," the God of Israel depicted in the Books of the Prophets "of the latter period of the Kingdoms of Israel and Judah, Hosea, Isaiah, Micah, Zachariah, etc. . . . is both national and universal. He is still the God of His Chosen People, Israel, but He is also the God of the whole world who judgeth and guideth all nations."[11]

Buddhist scriptures endorse familial relationships. For example, they prescribe various duties between children and parents, and husbands and wives. At the same time, the Buddha encouraged us to look beyond our bonds with members of our own family, nation, or race, and to acknowledge the limitations of these relationships. For example, he stated, "Relatives are no more closely united than travellers who for a while meet at an inn, and then part again, losing sight of each other. . . . We see relatives behave unkindly, while non-relatives may show us kindness. . . . Therefore it is unworthy of you to allow your mind to become preoccupied with thoughts of your relatives. In the Samsaric world there is no fixed division between your own people and other people." The same principles apply to love for our country, which, while a legitimate emotion, must be moderated by an awareness that all countries fall short morally: "If you should hit on the idea that this or that country is safe, prosperous, or fortunate, give it up, my friend, and do not entertain it in any way; for you ought to know that the world everywhere is ablaze with the fires of some faults or others. . . . However delightful, prosperous, and safe a country may appear to be, it should be recognized as a bad country if consumed by the defilements." In this connection, in the words of one scholar, Buddhist scriptures regard "racial feelings . . . national feelings . . . and egotism or personal and national pride" as subtle defilements of the human mind.[12]

Confucius affirmed in the Analects that we owe certain duties to our family members and to our country. He recommended respect for parents and siblings. Indeed, according to a passage in the Analects, the roots of humaneness lie in "filiality and fraternity"— that is, in fulfilling duties within our own family. And Confucius stated, "The ruler is a ruler, the minister is a minister, the father is a father, the son is a son."[13]

Nevertheless, other passages in the Analects, such as the one referring to human brotherhood, suggest that these duties are subordinate to a concern for all individuals as members of one human family. Moreover, Confucius asserted that the central virtue of *ren* or *rŭn* (humaneness) means that one should be "in his dwelling, respectful; in his responsibilities, assiduous; toward others, loyal— though one go even to the Yí or Dí, this cannot be cast away." Confucianism scholars Brooks and Brooks find in this saying a "claim of universality despite cultural variants."

The works of Mencius also suggest an emphasis on the ethical primacy of potentially global unity over other social relationships. Mencius stated that the carrying out by a prince of his "kindness of heart" toward his relatives "will suffice for the love and protection of all within the four seas," because others will seek to emulate his behavior. Mencius further affirmed that if a prince should fail to show kindness, then "he will not be able to protect his wife and children." These statements appear to assert that an important purpose and effect of showing kindness to relatives is to promote love for and the protection of all members of the human race in addition to our family members. Indeed, according to one twentieth-century scholar who has attempted to relate Confucian teachings to the present international order, the "rulers of the nations must promote the general welfare of mankind as the ultimate goal of the efforts of each national community."[14]

In the New Testament, some of St. Paul's letters as well as those of St. Peter recognize duties of obedience in particular social relationships—of wives to husbands, children to parents, and slaves to masters, among others. The New Testament also enjoins us to love and support our family. For example, according to St. Paul, "whoever does not provide for relatives, and especially for family members, has denied the faith and is worse than an unbeliever." And certain passages from the New Testament may endorse loyalty to states, such as Jesus's injunction to "give therefore to the emperor the things that are the emperor's, and to God the things that are

God's," and St. Paul's letter to the Romans, discussed later. But in light of Jesus's expansive definition of "neighbor" in the story of the Good Samaritan, and the teaching that we are to love all members of the human race as ourselves, these particular loyalties and duties could be understood as morally subordinate to a loyalty to and love for the entire human family. Indeed, one religion scholar has suggested that the New Testament's concern for human dignity arises out of dual emphases on "the unity of mankind" and a "'preferential option for the poor.'"[15]

There are passages in the Koran that recognize the legitimacy of different races and religious communities. But these passages exhort diverse nations and peoples to come together and cooperate: "O mankind, We have created you male and female, and appointed you races and tribes, that you may know one another. Surely the noblest among you in the sight of God is the most godfearing of you." The Koran affirms that "the variety of your tongues and hues" is an evidence of God. It endorses pluralism and collaboration among different peoples and religious groups to carry out good works: "If God had willed, He would have made you one nation; but that He may try you in what has come to you. So be you forward in good works; unto God shall you return, all together; and He will tell you of that whereon you were at variance." The Koran thus validates strong attachments to nations and religious communities within a framework of world unity. There are also specific provisions in the Koran, discussed in chapter 8, that support unity among members of the Muslim community while also permitting Jews and Christians to implement religious systems of their own.[16]

Finally, the Bahá'í writings endorse the legitimacy of identification with our family, nation, and religious community. But they simultaneously stress that we morally ought to recognize, above all, our membership in one human family. The Bahá'í writings thus emphasize that the central Bahá'í principle of the oneness of humankind

> can conflict with no legitimate allegiances, nor can it undermine
> essential loyalties. Its purpose is neither to stifle the flame of a
> sane and intelligent patriotism in men's hearts, nor to abolish
> the system of national autonomy so essential if the evils of ex-
> cessive centralization are to be avoided. It does not ignore, nor
> does it attempt to suppress, the diversity of ethnical origins, of
> climate, of history, of language and tradition, of thought and
> habit, that differentiate the peoples and nations of the world. It
> calls for a wider loyalty, for a larger aspiration than any that has
> animated the human race. . . . Its watchword is unity in diver-
> sity.[17]

# 3

## The Golden Rule
## and the Importance
## of Good Deeds

*In everything do to others as you would have them do to you; for this is the law and the prophets.*

—Jesus

# The Golden Rule

Most of the scriptures teach that we should treat others at least as well as, if not better than, we would want to be treated—a positive version of the Golden Rule. Some state that we have a minimal duty not to treat others as we would not want to be treated—a negative version of the Golden Rule. According to the scriptures, we owe this duty, in either its positive or negative formulation, to all human beings. A fair reading of the scriptures indicates an implied condition within the Golden Rule, however, that how we should want to be treated (and consequently should act towards others) ought to be determined by other substantive moral principles in the texts rather than by our individual preferences.[1]

With respect to particular scriptures, a scholar of the Bhagavad Gita has asserted that "one of the most striking and emphatic of the ethical doctrines of the Gītā is substantially that of the Golden Rule." He maintains that the Gita's articulation of the Golden Rule is grounded in its view of "the oneness of man with his neighbors and with God." For example, the Gita states, "By comparison with himself, in all (beings) / Whoso sees the same, Arjuna, / Whether it be pleasure or pain, / He is deemed the supreme disciplined man." And the Gita affirms that we should not harm others, because to do so would be to harm ourselves. This is because all of us manifest and are united in one God: "For seeing in all the same / Lord established, / He harms not himself (in others) by himself; / Then he goes to the highest goal."[2]

Many Jewish scholars have suggested that the Torah's most important ethical commandment is to "love your fellow as yourself." Rabbi Hillel later derived from this commandment a negative formulation of the Golden Rule: "'What you dislike don't do to others; that is the whole Torah. The rest is commentary. Go and learn.'" The Torah further teaches that God created humans in His own image, which means that our duty is to become like God—to cultivate His spiritual attributes. This teaching reflects a fundamental optimism that we can indeed develop spiritual virtues: "You shall be holy, for I, the Lord your God, am holy." It is furthermore a reason for us to treat others, who are also like God, with dignity and humaneness.[3]

Buddhist scriptures also reflect the Golden Rule. The Buddha affirmed, "Since to others, to each one for himself, the self is dear, therefore let him who desires his own advantage not harm another." Buddhism scholar Edward Conze interprets this passage as meaning that "we should cultivate our emotions so that we feel with others as if they were ourselves. If we allow the virtue of compassion to grow in us, it will not occur to us to harm anyone else, any more than we willingly harm ourselves."[4]

In the Analects Confucius advocated a negative formulation of the Golden Rule. When a companion of Confucius inquired, "is there one saying that one can put in practice in all circumstances?" Confucius answered, "That would be empathy, would it not? What he himself does not want, let him not do it to others." Confucius also taught the principle of *ren,* or *rŭn.* According to an apparently later portion of the Analects, Confucius defined *ren* as "loving others" and helping them: "You yourself want position, so you give position to others; you yourself want to advance, so you advance others. To be able to *take one's example from near at hand*—that can be said to be the method of *rén*." Even in putting ourselves in the place of another, however, we retain our "own cultivated judgment" about what is appropriate and do not simply adopt another's entire persona.[5]

Jesus identified the two most important commandments of the Hebrew scriptures as follows: "'You shall love the Lord your God with all your heart, and with all your soul, and with all your mind.' This is the greatest and first commandment. And a second is like it: 'You shall love your neighbor as yourself.' On these two commandments hang all the law and the prophets." He also taught, on the basis of these commandments, the Golden Rule: "In everything do to others as you would have them do to you; for this is the law and the prophets." Further, St. Paul exhorted all of us to view and treat others better than we view and treat ourselves: "Do nothing from selfish ambition or conceit, but in humility regard others as better than yourselves. Let each of you look not to your own interests, but to the interests of others." And he said, "Whenever we have an opportunity, let us work for the good of all."[6]

The Koran praises those who love "whosoever has emigrated to them," "preferring others above themselves, even though poverty be their portion." And the Bahá'í writings also teach the Golden Rule. Bahá'u'lláh affirmed that one who seeks truth "should not wish for others that which he doth not wish for himself." Moreover, he counseled, "If thine eyes be turned towards justice, choose thou for thy neighbour that which thou choosest for thyself." He further asserted, in explaining and praising the Koranic passage just quoted, "Blessed is he who preferreth his brother before himself."[7]

# The Importance of Good Deeds

All of the scriptures emphasize the imperative of carrying out good deeds and not only reflecting upon spiritual matters or speaking praiseworthy words. The Bhagavad Gita, for example, while lauding the virtues of meditation, encourages us to engage in meritorious actions as the essence of a spiritual attitude, declaring: "Worship originates in action." Furthermore, the Gita extols "virtuous deeds." A life of action is better than one of asceticism: "The man of discipline is higher than men of austerities." And the Gita criticizes "hypocrisy," that is, failing to put into action what we preach.[8]

The Hebrew scriptures also instruct us to undertake just deeds: "Justice, justice shall you pursue." And, as emphasized in more detail later, they specifically call upon rulers and all of us to rescue victims of human rights violations: "Rescue the wretched and the needy; save them from the hand of the wicked."[9]

The Buddha's teachings emphasize not only the cultivation of inner spirituality and a moral frame of mind—traditionally associated with Buddhist meditation—but also the carrying out of moral deeds. According to Buddhist scriptures, the Buddha exhorted us to "be energetic, persevere, and try to control your minds! Do good deeds, and try to win mindfulness!" The Buddha, like Krishna in the Bhagavad Gita, counseled us to reject asceticism, and instead to pursue a middle path between the extremes of self-deprivation and sensual indulgence. Confucius, too, affirmed that commendable actions are much more praiseworthy than pious declarations: "The gentleman is ashamed to have his words run beyond his deeds." And he asserted that if a person "sees what is right but does not do it, he lacks courage."[10]

In the New Testament, Jesus taught, through such stories as that of the Good Samaritan, that we must actively help others in need. And his formulation of the Golden Rule is also a counsel to perform virtuous deeds. Further, Jesus said that the people should not emulate the scribes and Pharisees, because they did not "practice what they teach."[11]

A number of passages in the Koran call for a struggle *(jihad)* in the path of God, requiring action (which may be nonviolent) and not mere words: "Such believers as sit at home—unless they have an injury—are not the equals of those who struggle in the path of God with their possessions and their selves." Bahá'u'lláh, too, emphasized that we should perform virtuous actions rather than simply utter meritorious words that fail to be confirmed by our deeds: "Beware . . . lest ye walk in the ways of them whose words differ from their deeds. . . . Let your acts be a guide unto all mankind, for the professions of most men, be they high or low, differ from their conduct." And 'Abdu'l-Bahá said, "The wrong in the world continues to exist just because people talk only of their ideals, and do not strive to put them into practice. If actions took the place of words, the world's misery would very soon be changed into comfort."[12]

# 4

## Personal Virtues and Moral Duties

*Fearlessness, purification of essence, / Steadfastness in the discipline of knowledge, / Generosity, control, and religious worship, / Study of the Holy Word, austerities, uprightness, / Harmlessness, truth, no anger, / Abandonment, serenity, no backbiting, / Compassion towards creatures, no greedy desire, / Gentleness, modesty, no fickleness, / Majesty, patience, fortitude, purity, / No injuriousness, no excessive pride, / Are (the qualities) of him that to the divine lot / Is born, son of Bharata.*
—Krishna

# Personal Virtues and Moral Duties in the Scriptures

All the scriptures prescribe particular personal virtues that we should cultivate, as well as moral duties that we owe to our fellow human beings. These virtues and duties include, among many others, kindness and compassion; generosity and unselfishness; help for the injured, the sick, the needy, and the oppressed; patience; forgiveness; peace and the nonuse of force in interpersonal relations; truthfulness; fidelity to promises; restraint in speech; humility; and justice and impartiality.

# Kindness and Compassion

Passages from all the scriptures call upon us to show kindness to one another. This is both a moral duty and a virtue. At the same time, many passages recognize that society cannot treat criminals or gross human rights violators kindly, but rather must treat them justly.

43

For example, the Bhagavad Gita praises the virtues of friendliness and "compassion towards creatures," including other members of the human family. The Torah enjoins Jews to show kindness and compassion not only to fellow Jews, but also to foreigners: "You shall not oppress a stranger, for you know the feelings of the stranger, having yourselves been strangers in the land of Egypt." According to Buddhist scriptures, the Buddha taught "to do no injury to any living being but to be full of love and kindness."[1]

In the Analects Confucius specifically praised kindness and magnanimity as virtues. However, when Confucius was asked by a companion, "Requite malice with kindness: how about that?" he answered, "With what then will you requite kindness? Requite malice with uprightness; requite kindness with kindness." This passage appears to affirm that wrongdoers should be treated with justice, rather than kindness.[2]

As noted in chapter 2, Mencius called upon princes (and indeed all individuals) to show "kindness of heart." Mencius later elaborated on the concept of humane treatment and our universal capacity for compassion for others. He cited as an example the natural response of alarm and distress that anyone seeing a child about to fall into a well would feel. We would have these feelings because of compassion rather than any desire for reward or enhanced reputation. Mencius affirmed, moreover, that since all men have the virtues of benevolence, righteousness, propriety, and knowledge in themselves, they should devote their full energies to the cultivation of these virtues, which when so developed "will suffice to love and protect all within the four seas." If men fail to develop these virtues, the virtues "will not suffice for a man to serve his parents with." In Mencius's view, therefore, according to a scholar of Confucianism, "becoming humane is within the competence of everyone and depends only on extending the affection and respect that are felt for those nearby in ever widening concentric circles of concern."[3]

In the New Testament Jesus encouraged us to show kindness and compassion toward all. He enjoined us to forgive others and to love even our enemies, for "if you greet only your brothers and sisters, what more are you doing than others?" He also counseled us to "turn the other cheek": "You have heard that it was said, 'An eye for an eye and a tooth for a tooth.' But I say to you, Do not resist an evildoer. But if anyone strikes you on the right cheek, turn the other also; and if anyone wants to sue you and take your coat, give your cloak as well; and if anyone forces you to go one mile, go also the second mile. Give to everyone who begs from you, and do not refuse anyone who wants to borrow from you." And St. Paul affirmed that the fruit of the Spirit includes "kindness" and "gentleness."[4]

The Koran counsels, "Be kind to . . . the neighbour who is of kin, and to the neighbour who is a stranger." 'Abdu'l-Bahá similarly extolled the virtues of kindness and compassion, calling on us to manifest "love and kindness to all humanity." But 'Abdu'l-Bahá also taught that criminals must not be treated mercifully: "Kindness cannot be shown the tyrant, the deceiver, or the thief, because, far from awakening them to the error of their ways, it maketh them to continue in their perversity as before."[5]

# Generosity and Unselfishness

All the scriptures endorse the virtues of generosity and unselfishness. The Gita prescribes generosity as a desirable virtue. Moreover, the Gita enjoins us to give to others, without any expectation of a benefit in return: "The gift which with the mere thought 'One must give!' / Is given to one that does no (return) favor, / At the proper place and time, to a worthy person, / That gift is said to be of goodness. / But what in order to get a return favor, / Or with a view to the fruit as well, / Or when it hurts to give, is given, / That gift is said to be of passion." Further, we should not act out of selfishness or self-interest: "Abandoning all desires, what / Man moves free from longing, / Without self-interest and egotism, / He goes to peace." The disciplined man is "No hater of all beings, / Friendly and compassionate, / Free from selfishness and I-faculty." And the Gita decries "Hoardings of wealth by wrong means."[6]

According to the Torah, one of God's commandments is to save the fallen fruit of one's vineyard for the poor and the stranger. Further, the Torah states, "If . . . there is a needy person among you, one of your kinsmen in any of your settlements in the land that the Lord your God is giving you, do not harden your heart and shut your hand against your needy kinsman. Rather, you must open your hand and lend him sufficient for whatever he needs." Property owners must set aside a portion of their land's food production for the benefit of the "stranger, the fatherless, and the widow." Proverbs affirms that we should treat even our enemies generously: "If your enemy is hungry, give him bread to eat; If he is thirsty, give him water to drink."[7]

According to Buddhist scriptures, the Buddha counseled, "Not to be helpful to others, Not to give to those in need, This is the fruit of Samsara [the world of birth and death]. Better than this is to renounce the idea of a self." He advised us to give voluntarily of our wealth to those less fortunate: "He who pursues wealth in a lawful way, and having done so gives freely of his wealth thus lawfully obtained,—by so giving, by making such sacrifices, he begets much merit." And Buddhist scriptures praise the virtue of "giving." The Buddha thus advocated a "responsibility to help others materially, intellectually, and spiritually."[8]

Confucius taught that leaders should be magnanimous in feeding the people and should "enrich them." The Analects also praises a ruler who "examined rules and standards," was generous, faithful, diligent and fair, and thus won over his people.[9]

According to the New Testament, Jesus proclaimed, as noted above, "Give to everyone who begs from you, and do not refuse anyone who wants to borrow from you." He instructed us to forego material treasures and desires in favor of righteousness and spiritual wealth, and to donate our possessions to the needy. And St. Paul praised the virtue of "generosity."[10]

The Koran states, "It is not piety, that you turn your faces to the East and to the West. True piety is this: to believe in God, and the Last Day, the angels, the Book, and the Prophets, to give of one's substance, however cherished, to kinsmen, and orphans, the needy, the traveller, beggars, and to ransom the slave, to perform the prayer, to pay the alms." We are to give food to the "needy, the orphan, the captive" out of love for God, and not out of any expectation of a reciprocal benefit or appreciation, saying: "'We feed you only for the Face of God; we desire no recompense from you, no thankfulness.'"[11]

Finally, the Bahá'í writings counsel, "Be generous in prosperity, and thankful in adversity. . . . Be a treasure to the poor, an admonisher to the rich, an answerer to the cry of the needy." They further assert that the true spiritual seeker should "succor the dispossessed, and never withhold his favor from the destitute."[12]

# Help for the Injured, the Sick, the Needy, and the Oppressed

A central theme of all the scriptures is the moral imperative of helping the injured, the sick, the needy, and the oppressed out of recognition of their membership in one human family. For example, the Bhagavad Gita states, as we have seen, that we should show "compassion towards creatures."[13]

The Hebrew scriptures exhort us to defend the rights of the poor and the oppressed: "Speak up for the dumb, For the rights of all the unfortunate. Speak up, judge righteously, Champion the poor and the needy." And Isaiah counsels, "Learn to do good. Devote yourselves to justice; Aid the wronged. Uphold the rights of the orphan; Defend the cause of the widow."[14]

As noted above, Buddhist scriptures as well as the Analects encourage assistance to those in need. Jesus likewise made clear that his message was one of concern for the poor, the sick, and the oppressed. He claimed to fulfill the prophecy of Isaiah and to be the one "to bring good news to the poor . . . to proclaim release to the captives and recovery of sight to the blind, to let the oppressed go free." In his Sermon on the Mount, he declared, "Blessed are the poor in spirit, for theirs is the kingdom of heaven. . . . Blessed are the meek, for they will inherit the earth. . . . Blessed are those who are persecuted for righteousness' sake, for theirs is the kingdom of heaven."[15]

The Koran lays down a duty to come to the rescue of people in distress. In this connection, it affirms, "How is it with you, that you do not fight in the way of God, and for the men, women, and children who, being abased, say, 'Our Lord, bring us forth from this city whose people are evildoers, and appoint to us a protector from Thee, and appoint to us from Thee a helper'?"[16]

The Bahá'í writings strongly emphasize duties to protect the rights of others and defend them against tyranny and oppression. For example, Bahá'u'lláh called upon all of us not to tolerate violations of human rights, including violations of the rights of women: "As [the friends of God] do not allow themselves to be the object of cruelty and transgression, in like manner they should not allow such tyranny to visit the handmaidens of God." And he instructed us to be "as a lamp unto them that walk in darkness, a joy to the sorrowful, a sea for the thirsty, a haven for the distressed, an upholder and defender of the victim of oppression."[17]

# Patience

All the scriptures extol the virtue of patience. The Bhagavad Gita counsels the cultivation of many personal virtues, including serenity, fortitude, and patience. Both Jews and Christians admire Job as an example of spiritual patience and fortitude in the face of adversity. In the Hebrew scriptures, Job proclaimed, "Until I die I will maintain my integrity. I persist in my righteousness and will not yield." Buddhist scriptures endorse as one of "six perfections" the virtue of patience. And they indicate that patience is one of the qualities required of those who proceed along the Holy Eight Fold Path. Confucius similarly encouraged fortitude and diligence. According to the Analects, a gentleman is "poised and unruffled; the little man is always in a dither."[18]

The New Testament lauds the virtues of patience and determination. In his letter to the Galatians, St. Paul said that "patience" is one of the fruits of the Spirit. And he exhorted, "So let us not grow weary in doing what is right, for we will reap at harvest time, if we do not give up." The Koran praises "he who bears patiently and is forgiving," and those who "endure with fortitude misfortune, hardship and peril." The Bahá'í writings indicate that the "true seeker" must "cling unto patience and resignation." Moreover, they affirm that our exaltation springs from our acquisition of virtues such as "fortitude."[19]

# Forgiveness

Passages from all the scriptures endorse the virtue of forgiveness by individuals. For example, the Bhagavad Gita venerates the virtues of "harmlessness," "no anger," and "no backbiting." The Torah condemns vengeance and encourages forgiveness: "You shall not take vengeance or bear a grudge against your countrymen." Buddhist scriptures counsel us to respond to perceived wrongs with love, not hatred: "'He abused me, he beat me, he defeated me, he robbed me'—in those who do not harbor such thoughts hatred will cease. For hatred does not cease by hatred at any time; hatred ceases by love—this is an eternal law." And in the Analects, a companion of Confucius speaks highly of a friend who was "wronged, yet not retaliating."[20]

We have seen that in the New Testament Jesus counseled us, "if anyone strikes you on the right cheek, turn the other also." He exhorted us to forgive the sins of others: "For if you forgive others their trespasses, your heavenly Father will also forgive you; but if you do not forgive others, neither will your Father forgive your trespasses." And again Jesus said, "Do not judge, so that you may not be judged. . . . Why do you see the speck in your neighbor's eye, but do not notice the log in your own eye?" St. Paul instructed, "Do not repay anyone evil for evil, but take thought for what is noble in the sight of all. If it is possible, so far as it depends on you, live peaceably with all. Beloved, never avenge yourselves, but leave room for the wrath of God; for it is written, 'Vengeance is mine, I will repay, says the Lord.'"[21]

The Koran calls for forgiveness in interpersonal relationships rather than retaliation. Citing the Mosaic injunction of a "life for a life," an "eye for an eye," and "for wounds retaliation," the Koran indicates that "whosoever forgoes it as a freewill offering, that shall be for him an expiation." Similarly, the Koran lauds those who "when they are angry forgive" and, as noted above, "he who bears patiently and is forgiving."[22]

'Abdu'l-Bahá encouraged us to pardon those who wrong us. He stated, "If some one commits an error and wrong toward you, you must instantly forgive him." And he further affirmed: "If one person assaults another, the injured one should forgive him." He clearly condemned vengeance: "Punishment is for the protection of man's rights, but it is not vengeance; vengeance appeases the anger of the heart by opposing one evil to another. This is not allowable."[23]

# Peace and the Nonuse of Force in Interpersonal Relations

Passages from all the scriptures support a general principle of peace and nonviolence in interpersonal relations. For example, the Bhagavad Gita endorses nonviolence and harmlessness (*ahimsā*). It encourages "gentleness" and "no injuriousness" and condemns those who are filled with "violence." These teachings have inspired many Hindu beliefs and, of course, Gandhi's advocacy of nonviolent social reform. Gandhi said the Gita was for him "an infallible guide of conduct."[24]

The Hebrew scriptures extol peace. The Torah states, "[May the] Lord bestow His favor upon you and grant you peace!" The Hebrew scriptures exhort us to "seek amity and pursue it." The injunction to love our neighbor as ourselves applies also to the treatment of foreigners: "The stranger who resides with you shall be to you as one of your citizens; you shall love him as yourself, for you were strangers in the land of Egypt." Furthermore, there is a strong bib-

lical injunction against murder. Indeed, according to later rabbinical interpreters, "one must not commit a murder even to save one's
own life." Other passages point to a fundamental ethic of nonviolence, and announce that might does not make right: "Not by might,
nor by power, but by My spirit—said the Lord of Hosts."[25]

One of the so-called "Five Precepts" of Buddhism, common to
all of the denominations, is "to abstain from taking life." And Buddhist scriptures praise the "sages who injure no one" and promote
peaceful conduct free from anger. Confucius taught that we should
strive for harmony, and avoid competition. In addition, the Analects
affirms that the gentleman "from the movements of his demeanor
. . . bans cruelty and arrogance." A gentleman "hates those who are
daring but violent." In our dealings with others we must respond
nonviolently to any injustices they may commit against us. The
Analects thus commends a person who was "wronged, yet not retaliating."[26]

The New Testament calls on us as individuals to practice peace
among one another. Jesus affirmed, "Blessed are the peacemakers,
for they will be called children of God." He said to us, "Peace I
leave with you; my peace I give to you." Jesus's conception of peace
apparently included abstention from violence whenever possible.
For example, when a follower took out a sword and struck the ear
of the slave of the high priest, Jesus admonished him, "Put your
sword back into its place; for all who take the sword will perish by
the sword." St. Paul counseled, "Live in harmony with one another;
do not be haughty, but associate with the lowly; do not claim to be
wiser than you are. Do not repay anyone evil for evil, but take
thought for what is noble in the sight of all. If it is possible, so far as
it depends on you, live peaceably with all."[27]

The Koran refers to itself as "a Book Manifest whereby God guides
whosoever follows His good pleasure in the ways of peace." Fur-

ther, it renews the instruction in the Hebrew scriptures not to kill another, except as punishment for crimes, and it upholds the immeasurable value of every person's life: "Therefore We prescribed for the Children of Israel that whoso slays a soul not to retaliate for a soul slain, nor for corruption done in the land, shall be as if he had slain mankind altogether; and whoso gives life to a soul, shall be as if he had given life to mankind altogether." And the Koran admonishes, "Kill not one another."[28]

Bahá'u'lláh stated, "Ye have been forbidden to commit murder." Moreover, the Bahá'í writings more generally prohibit conflict and aggression and encourage peace among individuals. For example, they declare, "O ye beloved of the Lord! In this sacred Dispensation, conflict and contention are in no wise permitted. Every aggressor deprives himself of God's grace." Further, 'Abdu'l-Bahá proclaimed, "When a thought of war comes, oppose it by a stronger thought of peace. A thought of hatred must be destroyed by a more powerful thought of love."[29]

# Truthfulness

All the scriptures require us to be truthful. Thus, the Bhagavad Gita lauds the virtue of "truth." It enjoins "austerity of speech," which means to speak words that are "true" as well as "pleasingly beneficial." One of the Ten Commandments in the Torah is "You shall not bear false witness against your neighbor." The Torah also states, "You shall not deal deceitfully or falsely with one another." And Proverbs declares, "Lying speech is an abomination to the Lord." Among the Five Precepts of Buddhism is "to abstain from false speech." The Buddha further instructed, "Speak the truth."

Confucius in the Analects praised fidelity: "A man, but without fidelity: I don't know if that can be. A large cart with no yoke, a small cart with no collar: how shall one make them go?"[30]

Jesus reaffirmed the Torah's teaching against false speech, explaining to his disciples, "What comes out of the mouth proceeds from the heart, and this is what defiles. For out of the heart come evil intentions, . . . false witness, slander. These are what defile a person." The Koran states, "O believers, fear God, and be with the truthful ones." And it condemns falsely blaming the innocent: "And whosoever earns a fault or a sin and then casts it upon the innocent, thereby has laid upon himself calumny and manifest sin." Bahá'u'lláh counseled, "Beautify your tongues, O people, with truthfulness, and adorn your souls with the ornament of honesty." The Bahá'í writings further affirm, "'Truthfulness is the foundation of all human virtues.'"[31]

# Fidelity to Promises

All the scriptures praise the virtue of fidelity to promises. For example, the Bhagavad Gita condemns "hypocrisy," implying that we should follow through with what we promise. According to the Torah, the promises of men are always binding: "If a man makes a vow to the Lord or takes an oath imposing an obligation on himself, he shall not break his pledge; he must carry out all that has crossed his lips." The Buddha also taught that we should make promises only in good faith: "When your solemn promises are made in all good faith, help will come from the love of the fairies." And Confucius instructed us to keep our promises: "First [the gentleman] carries out his words, and then he remains consistent with them." Further, the "gentleman wants to be slow in giving his word, but quick in carrying it out."[32]

In the New Testament, too, Jesus praised faithfulness to our word, including in safeguarding the property of another: "Whoever is faithful in a very little is faithful also in much; and whoever is dishonest in a very little is dishonest also in much. If then you have not been faithful with the dishonest wealth, who will entrust to you the true riches? And if you have not been faithful with what belongs to another, who will give you what is your own?"[33]

The Koran teaches that we should honor our promises: "And they who fulfil their covenant when they have engaged in a covenant . . . these are they who are true in their faith, these are the truly godfearing." Finally, Bahá'u'lláh affirmed that one should not "promise that which he doth not fulfill." He further stated that we should be a "'preserver of the sanctity'" of our pledge.[34]

# Restraint in Speech

The scriptures uniformly urge us to be restrained in our speech and to be respectful to our listeners. Many of them further condemn backbiting. For example, the Bhagavad Gita enjoins "truth, no anger, . . . [and] no backbiting," and it condemns "harshness (of speech)." The Torah states, "Do not deal basely with your countrymen." And a verse in Psalms praises a man "whose tongue is not given to evil."[35]

According to Buddhist scriptures, the Buddha counseled gentleness and honesty in speech: "Speak the truth; do not yield to anger; . . . Beware of the anger of the tongue, and control your tongue! Leave the sins of the tongue, and practice virtue with your tongue!" He further admonished, "Do not speak harshly to anyone; those who are spoken to will answer you in the same way. Angry speech is painful: blows for blows will touch you." Confucius likewise taught that in all endeavors, including speech, we should practice the "mean" and moderation: "The efficacy of the Middle Method, is it not the ultimate? But among the people it has long indeed been rare!"[36]

Jesus urged us not to backbite, but rather first to talk in private directly with the person whose behavior we believe needs correcting. Jesus stated, "If another member of the church sins against you, go and point out the fault when the two of you are alone. If the member listens to you, you have regained that one." James condemned malicious speech against others, and warned of its dangers: "And the tongue is a fire. . . . No one can tame the tongue—a restless evil, full of deadly poison. With it we bless the Lord and Father, and with it we curse those who are made in the likeness of God. From the same mouth come blessing and cursing. My brothers and sisters, this ought not to be so." St. Paul likewise criticized those who are "gossips" and "slanderers."[37]

The Koran prohibits backbiting, stating, "O believers, eschew much suspicion; some suspicion is a sin. And do not spy, neither backbite one another." Bahá'u'lláh counseled, "'Be . . . guarded in thy speech.'" He further affirmed, "A kindly tongue is the lodestone of the hearts of men." He prohibited backbiting, writing that "backbiting quencheth the light of the heart, and extinguisheth the life of the soul."[38]

# Humility

All the scriptures exhort us to be humble before others. The Bhagavad Gita repeatedly emphasizes that we should avoid "excessive pride" and "arrogance." And it criticizes those who are "self-conceited," "haughty," and "full of pride." The Hebrew scriptures affirm, "Pride goes before ruin, Arrogance, before failure. Better to be humble and among the lowly Than to share spoils with the proud."³⁹ Further, the teaching that we should love our neighbors as ourselves provides a reason for us to be humble to and respectful of all.

According to Buddhist scriptures, our search for truth requires humility and a willingness to ignore the faults of others in favor of tending to our own: "The fault of others is easily perceived, but that of one's self is difficult to perceive; a man winnows his neighbor's faults like chaff, but his own fault he hides, as a cheat hides an unlucky cast of the die. If a man looks after the faults of others and is always inclined to be offended, his own passions will grow, and he is far from the destruction of passion."⁴⁰

In the Analects Confucius taught that the gentleman loves learning. Learning involves an attitude of humility and an admission of the narrowness of our own knowledge. Indeed, part of knowing is to "regard knowing it as knowing it; to regard *not* knowing it as *not* knowing it." Confucianism scholars Brooks and Brooks interpret this passage as affirming that "true wisdom includes awareness of the limits of knowledge." Moreover, we should look at and seek to correct our own shortcomings instead of focusing on the shortcomings of others. Confucius declared, "To attack one's evils, but never attack the evils of others, is that not improving shortcomings?"⁴¹

Jesus counseled us to be humble, like a child. When the disciples asked him, "Who is the greatest in the kingdom of heaven?," he called a child and said, "Truly I tell you, unless you change and become like children, you will never enter the kingdom of heaven. Whoever becomes humble like this child is the greatest in the kingdom of heaven." And Jesus stated, "All who exalt themselves will be humbled, but all who humble themselves will be exalted." Likewise, St. Paul, in his letter to the Philippians, affirmed, "Do nothing from selfish ambition or conceit, but in humility regard others as better than yourselves."⁴²

The Koran prescribes humility: "Prosperous are the believers who in their prayers are humble and from idle talk turn away and at almsgiving are active." And the Koran asserts that we should "find not fault with one another." The Bahá'í writings state, "Humility exalteth man to the heaven of glory and power, whilst pride abaseth him to the depths of wretchedness and degradation." They also exhort us to focus on our own faults and overlook the faults of others: "Magnify not the faults of others that thine own faults may not appear great." They further counsel us, "Breathe not the sins of others so long as thou art thyself a sinner."[43]

# Justice and Impartiality

All the scriptures instruct us to be just and impartial. They imply that to be just and impartial means to adhere to moral principles, without regard to our self-interest or our family relationships. For example, the Bhagavad Gita counsels us to fulfill our duties to all human beings, even to our enemies, impartially, and with the same mental outlook: "To friend, ally, foe, remote neutral, / Holder of middle ground, object of enmity, and kinsman, / To good and evil men alike, / Who has the same mental attitude, is superior." The focus of our lives should be on moral action: "On action alone be thy interest, / Never on its fruits; Let not the fruits of action be thy motive, / Nor be thy attachment to inaction. Abiding in discipline perform actions, / Abandoning attachment, Dhanaṃjaya, / Being indifferent to success or failure; Discipline is defined as indifference." The indifference referred to in this passage relates to detachment from our own desires and self-interest.[44]

The Torah commands judges and rulers to "govern the people with due justice" and to demonstrate "no partiality." It counsels them to constantly pursue justice. The Torah affirms that judges must listen carefully to all parties to a case, and reach a decision on the basis of what is just, not based on a fear that they will be criticized: "You shall not be partial in judgment: hear out low and high alike. Fear no man, for judgment is God's." The Torah also indicates that all of us must not join the opinion of the majority if in doing so a wrong would be committed. The commentaries of the rabbis later asserted that judges can achieve fairness by putting themselves in the place of those whom they judge, in accordance with the Golden Rule. Further, all persons are equal before the law, and equal cases must be treated alike; indeed, there "shall be one law for the citizen and for the stranger who dwells among you."[45]

Buddhist scriptures require kings to behave impartially, and act based on what is just, as indicated by the following counsels to a king who is judging a lawsuit: "When a dispute arises he should pay equal attention to both parties to it, and hear the arguments of each and decide according to what is right. He should not . . . act out of favouritism, hatred, fear or folly." Moreover, according to one commentator, in Buddhist doctrine "justice demands consistency both in the statement of the law as well as in its application. But according to Buddhism consistency alone would not be a criterion of good law since the legal principles must conform with moral experience if the law is to promote justice rather than prevent or inhibit it."[46]

In the Analects Confucius exhorted us to covet virtue and not partiality. Indeed, the Analects asserts that we must conscientiously adhere to the virtuous path: "The gentleman's relation to the world is thus: he has no predilections or prohibitions. When he regards something as right, he sides with it." We should focus on what is right rather than self-interest: "The gentleman concentrates on right; the little man concentrates on advantage." Confucius rejected partisanship and small-mindedness: "The gentleman is broad and not partial; the little man is partial and not broad." Brooks and Brooks interpret this passage to mean that the "gentleman is consistent at the level of large principles; the little man, at that of precise loyalties." Further, Confucius exhorted us to "hold unto death to the Way of the Good" and to "stabilize [our] virtue." A gentleman should resolutely pursue humaneness without a concern for recognition by others; he should not "take it as a fault if others do not know him." Confucius went so far as to declare that the dedicated public servant and the principled man "may even bring about his own death in realizing *rén*." Similarly, Mencius later affirmed that while he liked both life and righteousness, if forced to make a choice between the two, he would choose righteousness.[47]

In the New Testament, Jesus called us to righteousness, asserting, "Unless your righteousness exceeds that of the scribes and Pharisees, you will never enter the kingdom of heaven." Jesus also declared that we are to be guided by love for him and by the high moral standards that he taught, rather than by love for our closest relatives, even our children: "Whosoever loves son or daughter more than me is not worthy of me; and whoever does not take up the cross and follow me is not worthy of me." And we have seen that he admonished us to love our enemies, effectively counseling us to treat them with the same respect that we would show to our friends. St. Paul suggested that God judges based on moral principles, not on our nationality or religion, for "God shows no partiality."[48]

The Koran calls upon us to observe justice in all our relationships. It affirms that we should act justly even when doing so could harm us or our family. The Koran asserts, "O believers, be you securers of justice, witnesses for God, even though it be against yourselves, or your parents and kinsmen, whether the man be rich or poor; God stands closest to either. Then follow not caprice, so as to swerve; for if you twist or turn, God is aware of the things you do." The Koran declares that we should be fair even in our dealings with those we dislike: "Let not detestation for a people move you not to be equitable; be equitable—that is nearer to godfearing."[49]

According to the Bahá'í writings, to do justice "is to give to everyone according to his deserts." 'Abdu'l-Bahá stated that justice within a country includes impartiality among citizens: "Kings must rule with wisdom and justice; prince, peer and peasant alike have equal rights to just treatment, there must be no favour shown to individuals. A judge must be no 'respecter of persons', but administer the law with strict impartiality in every case brought before him." 'Abdu'l-Bahá also said that to be just is "to have no regard for one's own personal benefits and selfish advantages, and to carry out the laws of God without the slightest concern for anything else. . . . It means to consider the welfare of the community as one's own."[50]

# 5

# The Equal Dignity of All Human Beings

*I do not call a man a brahmana because of his origin or of his mother. He is indeed arrogant, and he is wealthy: but the poor who is free from all attachments, him I call indeed a brahmana.*

—The Buddha

# Equal Human Dignity in the Scriptures

There are passages in all the sacred scriptures that regard human beings either as a divine creation, or as possessing the capacity for spiritual transformation, or both. According to the scriptures, then, everyone equally possesses an inherent spiritual dignity, regardless of our nationality, class, race, religion, or sex. The scriptures therefore affirm that none of us may legitimately be regarded as outsiders or as subhuman.

At the same time, the texts acknowledge that we differ in the degree to which we actually choose to exercise our capacities for moral development and behavior. And they also recognize certain moral limitations on the exercise of our freedoms arising from our moral duties. Nevertheless, the clear affirmation in many passages of the equal spiritual dignity of all human beings provides a solid foundation for recognizing the equal social dignity of all human beings as well.

# Hinduism and the Bhagavad Gita

The Bhagavad Gita suggests that in the sight of God all human beings are equal, regardless of caste or sex. What matters to God is our spiritual devotion. Krishna says, "I am the same to all beings, / No one is hateful or dear to Me; But those who revere Me with devotion, / They are in Me and I too am in them." And Krishna further states, "For if they take refuge in Me, son of Pṛthā, / Even those who may be of base origin, / Women, men of the artisan caste, and serfs too, / Even they go to the highest goal." The Gita also states repeatedly that we should treat all persons, whether of high or low caste, with the same consideration. As we saw in chapter 2, it affirms that the "wise see the same thing" in a Brahman and an outcaste. And it asserts, "Brahman-nirvāna is won / By the seers. . . . / Who delight in the welfare of all beings."[1]

Furthermore, the Gita implies that we can transcend our caste birth through spiritual detachment. According to one scholar, "One's access to the most important goal of salvation . . . is not . . . at all conditional on class or gender." For example, the Gita states, "Right in this world they have overcome birth, / Whose mind is fixed in indifference; For Brahman is flawless and indifferent; Therefore they are fixed in Brahman."[2]

Of course, cultural Hinduism has recognized the division of humanity into four castes or classes and many subgroups, in turn divided into clans and families, each with its own duties or dharma. Although the caste system is associated with Hindu culture and justified by certain passages from the Bhagavad Gita, there are other passages in the Gita that many interpreters believe suggest the illegitimacy of such a rigid hierarchical system. These passages include those discussed above that teach that we should treat all other human beings with the same consideration, regardless of their caste. A number of contemporary interpreters have argued accordingly that the Gita's egalitarian ethic does not support the caste system, and that its references to the caste system must be interpreted in light of this core principle.[3]

# Judaism and the
# Hebrew Scriptures

According to the story of Genesis in the Torah, God created human beings in His own image. This implies that all of us have a duty to acquire God's spiritual attributes. Furthermore, this teaching suggests that we have a duty to treat all other human beings with kindness and love because they, too, are created in the image of God. The Torah contains many admonitions to Jews to behave toward foreigners and members of other religions with the same respect due to a fellow Jew. Jews are enjoined to treat foreigners living in their midst as equal under the law: "You shall have one standard for stranger and citizen alike." Moreover, the Torah encourages Jews to feel emotional empathy for foreigners and to respect their liberty: "You shall not oppress a stranger, for you know the feelings of the stranger, having yourselves been strangers in the land of Egypt." Later rabbinical commentators held that Christians and Muslims were to be regarded as "strangers" entitled to the same love and respect as Jews. As we saw in Chapter 4, even enemies are to be treated humanely and with kindness. Nevertheless, much rabbinical law allowed various forms of discrimination against non-Jews and aliens.[4]

# Buddhism and
# Buddhist Scriptures

Buddhist scriptures emphasize that all human beings are members of one biological species. Moreover, the Buddha's teachings affirm the equal spiritual capacities of individuals representing all castes. He rejected any inborn special spiritual status for the caste of Hindu priests, or *brahmins*. According to Buddhist scriptures, our dignity is determined not by our social status at birth, but rather by our quest for spiritual perfections. The Buddha thus asserted, "I do not call a man a brahmana because of his origin or of his mother. He is indeed arrogant, and he is wealthy: but the poor who is free from all attachments, him I call indeed a brahmana."[5]

# Confucianism, the Analects, and the Works of Mencius

According to the Analects, what is most important is how we live our lives, not the station of our birth: "By nature they are near each other; by habitual action they become farther apart." Further, "It is the highest wisdom and the lowest stupidity that do not change." Confucianism scholar Irene Bloom argues that the first saying signifies both a "conviction of a fundamental similarity among human beings and the perception that individuals distinguish themselves through their personal development." These and other passages suggest that a strong sense of the essential equality of human beings pervades the teachings of Confucius and Mencius. Nevertheless, Confucius drew distinctions among people based on their degree of learning and ability to study: "Those who know it from birth are the highest, those who know it from study are next, those who despite difficulties study it are next after that. Those who in difficulties do *not* study: these are the lowest." But according to Irene Bloom the "gentleman" "is so designated solely on the basis of his nobility of personality rather than nobility of birth." Further, in Mencius's view, in addition to respect for others in a special relationship to ourselves—parents, for example, or rulers—there is always, in the words of the same scholar, a "basic respect required from each human being toward every other human being as a condition of their common humanity."[6]

# Christianity and the New Testament

According to the New Testament, Jesus showed special concern for the least fortunate, thereby affirming their equal human dignity. Indeed, he asserted that benevolent acts performed for the lowliest of society were accounted in the sight of God as performed for the Son of Man. He stated that when "the Son of Man comes in his glory," the righteous will ask of him, "Lord, when was it that we saw you hungry and gave you food, or thirsty and gave you something to drink? And when was it that we saw you a stranger and welcomed you, or naked and gave you clothing? And when was it that we saw you sick or in prison and visited you?" And he said that the Son of Man will answer them: "Truly I tell you, just as you did it to one of the least of these who are members of my family, you did it to me."[7]

There are, of course, as we have seen, many passages in the New Testament, particularly in the letters of St. Paul and St. Peter, that establish various social duties of obedience in special relationships, including the relationship between slaves and masters. Some commentators believe that these and other codes of conduct apparently at odds with the concept of equality were in fact inspired by Greek thought rather than directly by the words of Jesus. In any case, the superior parties in these relationships are to act justly. For example, St. Paul exhorted masters to treat their slaves "justly and fairly."[8]

# Islam and the Koran

As we noted in chapter 2, the Koran, like the Torah, asserts that all of us have an equal dignity as children of a single soul, and a hadith affirms that human beings are as "alike as the teeth of a comb." Passages from the Koran repeatedly imply the fundamental equality of all people, including members of different races and of both sexes. And in his Farewell Sermon, Muḥammad declared, "All of you come from Adam, and Adam is of dust. Indeed, the Arab is not superior to the non-Arab, and the non-Arab is not superior to the Arab. Nor is the fair-skinned superior to the dark-skinned nor the dark-skinned superior to the fair-skinned: superiority comes from piety and the noblest among you is the most pious."[9]

# The Baháʼí Faith and the Baháʼí Writings

The Baháʼí writings call for the elimination of all forms of prejudice and discrimination. According to ʻAbduʼl-Bahá, "In the estimation of God all men are equal; there is no distinction or preferment for any soul in the dominion of His justice and equity." The Baháʼí writings also affirm the equality of the races and require all of us to overcome deeply-ingrained racial stereotypes and prejudices. Baháʼuʼlláh advised us, "Close your eyes to racial differences, and welcome all with the light of oneness." And ʻAbduʼl-Bahá stated, "'Color is not important; the heart is all-important.'"[10]

# 6

# Human Rights

*Do we not have the right to our food and drink? . . . If we have sown spiritual good among you, is it too much if we reap your material benefits? If others share this rightful claim on you, do not we still more? Nevertheless, we have not made use of this right, but we endure anything rather than put an obstacle in the way of the gospel of Christ.*

—St. Paul

# Human Rights in the Scriptures

Passages from all of the scriptures recognize that we all have strong duties toward our fellow human beings and that we have an obligation to promote their human dignity and welfare. As we saw in Chapter 4, we owe special duties to the impoverished, the injured, the vulnerable, and victims of oppression or tyranny. Further, many of the texts positively call on us to come to the aid of others in defense of their rights.

Specific and fundamental duties that we owe to all other human beings and that are intended to benefit them directly can help establish substantive human rights to those benefits. And it is appropriate to recognize rights based on universal duties where individuals have the liberty to demand that others fulfill these duties to them.

Regardless of whether or not human rights can be inferred directly from the moral duties recognized in the scriptures, it is at least clear that these duties and the scriptures' moral teachings promote human dignity and therefore are consistent with and have historically influenced the concept of universal human rights. One political scientist has asserted in this connection that "the historical foundation of human rights lies in the humanist strand running throughout the world's great religions."[1]

At a minimum, the rights implied in the scriptures encompass the right to life, freedom from physical harm, and a minimal stan-

73

dard of subsistence, including adequate food, shelter, and clothing. They also include freedom of religion and conscience. These specific rights will be explored in subsequent chapters. The remainder of this chapter deals with human rights more generally in the scriptures of each religion.

# Hinduism and the Bhagavad Gita

As we saw in Chapter 4, the Bhagavad Gita instructs us to cultivate many personal virtues and to carry out many duties for the benefit of others. These include generosity and unselfishness, compassion toward creatures, harmlessness (*ahimsā*), gentleness and the nonuse of force, and restraint in speech and abstention from backbiting. Although the Gita does not invoke the concept of "human rights" explicitly, it does recognize that these are strong duties, many of which are intended by Krishna directly to benefit our fellow human beings. For example, the Gita affirms that we should "delight in the welfare of all beings." These duties thereby provide a basis for recognizing universal human rights.[2]

# Judaism and the Hebrew Scriptures

According to the Hebrew scriptures, the Ten Commandments include instructions to honor our father and mother, and to desist from murder, adultery, theft, perjury, and sexual infidelity. Other commandments are to save fallen fruit for the poor and the stranger; to treat and judge fellow human beings fairly; and to treat a stranger as a fellow citizen and love him as ourselves. Under rabbinical law, at least seven Noachide commandments apply to non-Jews as well as Jews. These are the prohibitions of idolatry, blasphemy, murder, adultery, robbery, and eating from a living animal, and the obligation to establish courts of justice. Religion scholar Michael Fishbane concludes that the Noachide covenant "provides an ancient minimal statement on human rights. It protects humans from certain nonsocial behaviors and even guarantees protection under the law."[3]

Of course, the Hebrew scriptures do not speak in terms of "rights," but rather duties. A reading of the Hebrew scriptures in context demonstrates, however, that many of the duties they prescribe, including a number of the Ten Commandments, are intended by God to be strict duties and to benefit other human beings directly. As recognized by certain scholars, these duties therefore give rise to some substantive human rights. Further, the Hebrew scriptures call upon us courageously to defend the rights of our vulnerable brothers and sisters in the human family: "Speak up for the dumb, For the rights of all the unfortunate. Speak up, judge righteously, Champion the poor and the needy." Indeed, the prophet Isaiah foretold the liberation of all those who are oppressed. According to Isaiah, the Savior would appear as a "herald of joy to the humble, To bind up the wounded of heart, To proclaim release to the captives, Liberation to the imprisoned." The ultimate vision of the Hebrew scriptures, then, might be understood to be one of final redemption for victims of human rights violations.[4]

# Buddhism and Buddhist Scriptures

Buddhist scriptures lay down the Five Precepts of Buddhism, common to all of the denominations. These include observance of the rules "to abstain from taking life; to abstain from taking what is not given; to abstain from sensuous misconduct; to abstain from false speech; [and] to abstain from intoxicants as tending to cloud the mind." We must act to improve the welfare of our fellow human beings: "The fair tree of thought that knows no duality, Spreads through the triple world. It bears the flower and fruit of compassion, And its name is service of others." Another passage reads, "Not to be helpful to others, Not to give to those in need, This is the fruit of Samsara [the world of birth and death]. Better than this is to renounce the idea of a self."[5]

Again, there is no reference to "human rights" as such in Buddhist scriptures. And it is often said that the idea of human rights is alien to Buddhism because of the Buddhist concept of selflessness or "no-self." But this concept appears to refer to the desirability of detaching ourselves from self-oriented material pursuits and helping others—including protecting their rights. Furthermore, while the doctrine of no-self may imply that morally it may be preferable for us voluntarily to refrain from claiming all of our rights, Buddhist scriptures do not apparently prohibit us from doing so. Accordingly, many scholars of Buddhism today believe that Buddhist scriptures support respect for human rights. For example, according to religion scholar Taitetsu Unno, in Buddhism "respect for the individual and the recognition of rights is not a static but a dynamic fact which makes it imperative that as we affirm our own individual rights we must also be willing to give up ourselves in order to affirm the rights of others."[6]

# Confucianism, the Analects, and the Works of Mencius

In the Analects, Confucius, in addition to praising certain virtues, identified duties that we owe to others, including a duty to treat others humanely. As many modern-day scholars of Confucianism have pointed out, the Confucianism developed in the Analects and the works of Mencius has a strong individual-oriented emphasis consistent with recognition of universal human rights. In the words of Irene Bloom, "each individual, appreciating the humanity of others on the basis of his own humanity, has the duty to recognize and treat every other individual as fully human. Each individual has the corresponding 'right' to be recognized and treated as human." For example, the Analects implies that we all have a right to exercise our individual will: "The Three Armies can be deprived of their leader, but a common man cannot be deprived of his will." Confucianism scholars Brooks and Brooks find in this affirmation "that even a humble fellow's 'will' is inalienable . . . the strongest statement so far [in the Analects] of what a modern reader might call individual rights." And there appears to be nothing in the Analects or the works of Mencius that forbids us from claiming or demanding the human rights that Confucius's teachings implicitly recognize.[7]

# Christianity and the New Testament

Jesus reaffirmed many of the Ten Commandments. When asked by a young man which commandments he should keep, Jesus replied, "You shall not murder; You shall not commit adultery; You shall not steal; You shall not bear false witness; Honor your father and mother; also, You shall love your neighbor as yourself." We have seen that he prescribed many other moral duties owed to others as well.[8]

Many of the duties identified by Jesus support the concept of human rights. But Christian teachings also imply that morally we should not always exercise our rights. St. Paul states, "In fact, to have lawsuits at all with one another is already a defeat for you.

Why not rather be wronged? Why not rather be defrauded?" This might be seen as contradicting the notion of rights, except that St. Paul is counseling us voluntarily to forego the enforcement of our rights—a position that at least acknowledges that we have rights that *could* be claimed.[9]

Indeed, St. Paul himself asks Christian communities on behalf of himself and Barnabas, "Do we not have the right to our food and drink?" And again he asks, "If we have sown spiritual good among you, is it too much if we reap your material benefits? If others share this rightful claim on you, do not we still more? Nevertheless, we have not made use of this right, but we endure anything rather than put an obstacle in the way of the gospel of Christ." Furthermore, there are examples of Jesus claiming rights and protesting violations. For example, when Jesus was being interrogated by the high priest and was slapped on the face by a guard, he said, "If I have spoken wrongly, testify to the wrong. But if I have spoken rightly, why do you strike me?"[10]

# Islam and the Koran

The Koran lays down many duties toward others, including duties to respect their lives and security and to provide aid to the needy. These universal duties owed to all imply certain fundamental human rights. As elaborated in later chapters, these include rights to life, personal security, and economic subsistence. And much of the Koran emphasizes individual responsibility and our freedom to seek spiritual truth.[11] The Koran also apparently prohibits discrimination based on race, nationality, sex, and even religion in the enjoyment of these basic rights.

Western scholars often contend that such rights as may exist under Islam are limited to Muslims. The doctrine of jihad, described in Chapter 14, may seem to support this contention. And it is no doubt true that some Muslim leaders have often employed discriminatory doctrines to divest nonbelievers of some of the most fundamental of their rights, including the right to life. However, another interpretation of jihad views it as only authorizing defensive war, and therefore as calling for equal and humane treatment of non-Muslims who do not attack Muslims. Further, the Koranic passages quoted in chapter 4 suggest that non-Muslims as well as Muslims are entitled to benefit from the universal duties described in these passages.[12]

# The Bahá'í Faith and the Bahá'í Writings

The Bahá'í writings clearly state that fundamental human rights should be upheld by all people, at all times. For example, in numerous passages the Bahá'í scriptures stress the pervasiveness of human rights violations by governments. In the words of 'Abdu'l-Bahá, "kings and rulers have been able to control millions of human beings and have exercised that dominion with the utmost despotism and tyranny." This reality must be transformed, according to the Bahá'í writings, through the adoption and implementation of international human rights standards. In this connection, 'Abdu'l-Bahá stated, "Bahá'u'lláh taught that an equal standard of human rights must be recognized and adopted." And the Bahá'í writings assert that one essential element of human perfection is to "have regard for the rights of others."[13]

The Bahá'í writings, in addition to recognizing many particular human rights, emphasize the importance of judicial remedies for human rights violations. Thus, for example, 'Abdu'l-Bahá indicated that the spread of religious faith and literacy among the people would allow them to file applications with local authorities to "secure their rights," and that if they are not justly treated by those authorities, they should have the right to appeal their cases to higher courts.[14]

# 7

## The Right to Life, Physical Security, and Subsistence

*You are there to* govern; *what use have you for* killing? *If you desire the good, the people will be good.*

—Confucius

# The Right to Life and Physical Security

Passages from all the scriptures prohibit the unjust killing of a human being by individuals or governments, as well as the infliction of other assaults upon an individual's personal security. Further, many of the scriptures lay down procedural safeguards for a person accused of criminal acts. These duties to refrain from killing or harming another person and to protect the physical security of a person accused of crime are obligations owed to all human beings. The scriptures therefore implicitly recognize a right to life and physical security.

For example, the Bhagavad Gita asserts that people who take pride in murdering an enemy, gloating "'Yonder enemy has been slain by me, / And I shall slay others too'" will "fall to a foul hell."[1] This passage clearly condemns arbitrary killing, even of enemies.

The Torah outlaws murder, and its teaching that God created humans in His image could be understood to hold that human life is of absolute and immeasurable worth. Exodus forbids us to "bring death on those who are innocent and in the right." The Torah establishes a number of specific criminal procedural protections. For example, in order for a person accused of murder to be executed, more than one witness must provide evidence of his crime. The testimony of a single witness does not suffice, thus making few murder cases eligible for the death penalty. And according to later prophets such as Ezekiel, we are responsible as individuals before

83

the law for our crimes, a responsibility that can never be displaced onto another: "A child shall not share the burden of a parent's guilt, nor shall a parent share the burden of a child's guilt; the righteousness of the righteous shall be accounted to him alone, and the wickedness of the wicked shall be accounted to him alone." This conception of individual responsibility replaced earlier notions of intergenerational guilt appearing in the Torah.[2]

In the Torah, a general principle of punishment is based on reciprocity as fairness: "If anyone maims his fellow, as he has done so shall it be done to him: fracture for fracture, eye for eye, tooth for tooth. The injury he inflicted on another shall be inflicted on him." If this rule may seem harsh in some cases, it also requires that the punishment be proportionate to the injury inflicted by the crime and not be excessive. And as we saw in Chapter 4, it is accompanied by explicit prohibitions against the taking of vengeance. Further, Talmudic law later replaced these sanctions with monetary compensation.[3]

The Buddha prohibited us from killing or engaging in arms sales. He also required that individuals be granted various procedural protections in the determination of their guilt and an appropriate punishment. For example, each person charged had the right to a fair trial with specific legal protections.[4]

According to the Analects, the gentleman "from the movements of his demeanor . . . bans cruelty and arrogance." In keeping with the duty of governments to promote the interests of the governed, Confucius taught that leaders should not kill those "who have not the Way in order to uphold those who have the Way." He explained, "You are there to *govern*; what use have you for *killing*? If you desire the good, the people will be good." He also insisted that leaders should not commit or allow cruelty or killing: "If good men ran the state for a hundred years, one could finally rise above cruelty and abolish killing—true indeed is this saying!"[5]

We have seen that Jesus validated the Torah's commandment that "You shall not murder." His conduct also implies that he would approve of the granting of minimal procedural safeguards to persons accused of crimes. For example, Jesus demanded that the guard of the high priest refrain from lodging unjust accusations against him and wrongfully striking him. He also insisted that the scribes and Pharisees not neglect justice. Moreover, the New Testament implies that individuals can be punished only for their own crimes. According to one commentator, the "New Testament takes as given the affirmation of individual responsibility for wrongdoing that is found in Ezekiel 18."[6]

As we have noted, the Koran also reaffirms the Torah's instruction not to take the life of another. It allows for exceptions only in the case of punishment for murder or other crimes. Moreover, the Koran insists on the inestimable value of each of our lives.[7]

The Koran recognizes individual responsibility for criminal conduct, based on Koranic verses like the following: "Whosoever does evil shall be recompensed for it." But it provides a number of protections against unjust criminal punishments. For example, the Koran includes, according to scholar Abdulaziz Sachedina, the Torah's "'eye for an eye' limit on retaliation, although such retaliation is not commanded but merely permitted. . . . There are four purposes of punishment in Islamic criminal law: prevention, deterrence, retribution/revenge, and rehabilitation through repentance as a process of self-purification for one's crime." At the same time, there are verses in the Koran suggesting that it is always better to forgive than to exercise a right of retaliation. In addition, according to one contemporary scholar, Islamic criminal law requires a "measured response" that is not merely "the thoughtless impulse of revenge."[8]

Finally, we have seen that Bahá'u'lláh affirmed, "Ye have been forbidden to commit murder." Further, 'Abdu'l-Bahá stated that "murder, theft, treachery, falsehood, hypocrisy and cruelty are evil and reprehensible. . . . If [a man] commits a murder, he will be responsible." 'Abdu'l-Bahá also asserted that all people, whatever their social status, and apparently including individuals accused of a crime, have "equal rights to just treatment."[9]

# The Right to Subsistence

Passages from the scriptures imply that all of us, as well as our governments, have strong moral obligations to help the poor and to provide them with adequate food, clothing, shelter, and the other basic necessities of life. These obligations can help establish a right to subsistence.

For example, the Bhagavad Gita teaches that all of us have a duty to give to others without expecting a benefit in return. And the Gita lauds individuals who delight "in the welfare of all beings," who are "compassionate," and who exhibit "generosity." As we explored in Chapter 4, various commandments in the Hebrew scriptures also require the provision of assistance to the needy. Some scholars maintain that these commandments establish entitlements of the poor and not simply charitable obligations. Buddhist scriptures similarly teach that the wealthy should give to the poor, and as we will see in chapter 10, that kings have a duty to provide for the economic welfare of their people. In the Analects Confucius instructed leaders to safeguard the welfare of the people, including by providing them with sufficient food.[10]

As we have seen, Jesus counseled us to distribute our possessions to the less fortunate. And St. Paul asked, "Do we not have the right to our food and drink?" The Koran apparently acknowledges economic rights. It declares that "the beggar and the outcast" must have a share of the property of believers. The law of *zakat* implements these rights by requiring Muslims to transfer a prescribed portion of their wealth to the needy.[11]

Finally, the Bahá'í writings explicitly uphold a right to subsistence. 'Abdu'l-Bahá asserted, "Every human being has the right to live; they have a right to rest, and to a certain amount of well-being. As a rich man is able to live in his palace surrounded by luxury and the greatest comfort, so should a poor man be able to have the necessaries of life. Nobody should die of hunger; everybody should have sufficient clothing; one man should not live in excess while another has no possible means of existence." The Bahá'í writings make clear that extremes of poverty must be eliminated through "legislative readjustment of conditions" as well as voluntary giving, thus endorsing legal recognition of certain minimal economic rights.[12]

# 8

## The Right to Freedom of Religion and Conscience

*To you your religion, and to me my religion!*

—The Koran

# Freedom of Religion and Conscience in the Scriptures

All the scriptures acknowledge the right and responsibility of every one of us to exercise our mental and spiritual capacities in the pursuit of the truth, the acquisition of virtues, and the carrying out of moral duties. They also emphasize that we must each voluntarily choose our own life path within the framework of this right and responsibility. Passages from many scriptures, in fact, explicitly advocate freedom of religious belief and the cultivation of amicable relations among different religious communities. They recognize that faith and a moral conscience cannot be compelled. They thus endorse freedom of religion and conscience.

# Hinduism and the Bhagavad Gita

In the Bhagavad Gita Krishna counsels Arjuna to pursue "truth" and "knowledge"—a counsel that might open the door to the application of reason, as well as more intuitive and experiential forms of perception, in solving ethical problems: "The man of faith gets knowledge, / Intent solely upon it, restraining his senses. Having got knowledge, to supreme peace / In no long time he goes." By contrast, "darkness is born of ignorance." Moreover, the paths of reason and discipline both lead to truth. Indeed, the best path is one that combines knowledge and discipline: "Of these the possessor of knowledge, constantly disciplined, / Of single devotion, is the best."[1] The Gita's emphasis on the cultivation of spiritual virtues points to a notion of individual moral responsibility and moral choice.

Further, the Gita is sympathetic toward other religions such as the established Vedic cult. And some contemporary interpreters of the Gita believe that it teaches religious tolerance and the essential unity of moral values in all religions. According to one scholar, these principles led Hindu religious thought in India to develop "a firm tradition of universalism—the idea that all the various religious forms represent diverse paths to the one Truth, paths that are all in some degree valid."[2]

# Judaism and the Hebrew Scriptures

A number of passages in the Hebrew scriptures suggest that faith is primarily a matter of individual conscience. For example, the Ten Commandments are addressed to each of us as individuals. The Torah implies that we must exercise our own volition in following God's commandments and laws. According to later Jewish prophets, we should pursue learning and the acquisition of wisdom and understanding. The objective of seeking moral truth provides a foundation for a principle of freedom of expression—subject to certain moral prohibitions, such as against slander and blasphemy. This principle is reflected in Job: "On my part, I will not speak with restraint; I will give voice to the anguish of my spirit; I will complain in the bitterness of my soul." Nevertheless, the Hebrew scriptures also counsel us not to turn to other gods, and prescribe the penalty of death for those who attempt to dissuade others from the worship of God or who commit blasphemy. But some Jewish commentators point out that these laws all prohibit certain actions and that the Hebrew scriptures nowhere provide for punishment for incorrect beliefs, as such. Moreover, the study of the Talmud, a revered work of Jewish religious literature, was fundamentally an exercise in independent investigation and understanding.[3]

# Buddhism and Buddhist Scriptures

According to Buddhist scriptures, the Buddha sought to "break the monopolistic grip of the *brahmins* on religious teachings" by exhorting us to investigate religious verities for ourselves. He stated, "Hold fast to the truth as a lamp. Seek salvation alone in the truth. Look not for assistance to any one besides yourselves." And again he affirmed, "Do not ye go by hearsay, nor by what is handed down by others, nor by what people say, nor by what is stated on the authority of your traditional teachings. . . . But . . . when you know of yourselves: 'These teachings are not good . . . these teachings, when followed out and put in practice, conduce to loss and suffering'—then reject them." The ultimate goal is to be "freed by knowledge of the truth," and only each of us can pursue the truth for ourselves. Buddhist scriptures suggest that we should be open-minded about other religions, because all reveal the same truth. For example, a venerated Buddhist text, Saraha's "Treasury of Songs," recites that "there is one Lord revealed in many scriptures."[4]

# Confucianism and
# the Analects

In the Analects Confucius suggested that we must cultivate an inner love of learning, and learn for ourselves, for learning cannot be compelled. He said of his students: "If they are not eager, I don't expound. If they are not urgent, I don't explain. If I give out one corner and they don't come back with three corners, then I don't go on." Even the individual will of a common person is to be protected: "The Three Armies can be deprived of their leader, but a common man cannot be deprived of his will."[5]

Furthermore, learning involves self-reflection: "If he studies and does not reflect, he will be rigid. If he reflects but does not study, he will be shaky." And according to a later passage reporting the words of a follower of Confucius: "To be of wide learning and sincere intent, to question incisively and reflect on what is close at hand—*rén* will be found in this." These passages imply that we should not simply accept the authority of traditional teachings, but should also utilize our individual insight and innate moral sensibility.[6]

# Christianity and
# the New Testament

The New Testament can also be read as stressing the concept of freedom of conscience. Jesus's call to repentance is addressed fundamentally to us as individuals. He challenged us to ascertain the truth of his teachings for ourselves through an inner quest to discover and follow God's will: "Anyone who resolves to do the will of

God will know whether the teaching is from God or whether I am speaking on my own." Jesus's own conduct offered many examples of his respect for followers of diverse religions. These include his praise of the "Good Samaritan," who, as a Samaritan, was regarded by Jews as a heretic. They also include his encounter at Jacob's well with a Samaritan woman, who questioned why a Jew would ask a drink of a Samaritan, because "Jews do not share things in common with Samaritans."[7]

Similarly, St. Paul's speech to the Athenians manifests respect for other religions, an awareness of the essential unity of nations and religions, and a vision of individual search for spiritual truth: "Athenians, I see how extremely religious you are in every way. . . . From one ancestor [God] made all nations to inhabit the whole earth, and he allotted the times of their existence and the boundaries of the places where they would live, so that they would search for God and perhaps grope for him and find him—though indeed he is not far from each one of us. For 'In him we live and move and have our being'; as even some of your own poets have said, 'For we too are his offspring.'" St. Paul also suggested that we have an innate sense of conscience which is consistent with moral and divine law. Speaking of the Gentiles, he affirmed that "what the law requires is written on their hearts, to which their own conscience also bears witness."[8]

In his letter to the Romans, St. Paul instructed us to refrain from judging others, including people of other faiths, because God will judge all of us on the basis of our conduct, "the Jew first and also the Greek," for "God shows no partiality." And in Hebrews we find a recognition of the divine origin of prophets before Jesus: "Long ago God spoke to our ancestors in many and various ways by the prophets, but in these last days he has spoken to us by a Son."[9]

# Islam and the Koran

The Koran teaches that our religious faith is personal, and that we must voluntarily choose to turn toward God and His Prophets. It explicitly affirms that no one has a right to force us to become members of a particular religion, including Islam: "No compulsion is there in religion." It states further, "And if thy Lord had willed, whoever is in the earth would have believed, all of them, all together. Wouldst thou then constrain the people, until they are believers? It is not for any soul to believe save by the leave of God." The Koran also instructs, "'The truth is from your Lord; so let whosoever will believe, and let whosoever will disbelieve.'"[10]

At the same time, many Koranic passages indicate that Islam is the true path to God. There are Koranic verses stating that if believers leave the path of Islam, they will suffer spiritually. For example, the Koran states, "Surely those who disbelieve after they have believed and then increase in unbelief—their repentance shall not be accepted; those are the ones who stray." There are hadiths suggesting that apostates should be punished by death. Many scholars and commentators, however, emphasize that the Koran itself does not prescribe any earthly punishment for "non-profession or renunciation of faith."[11]

The Koran affirms that Muslims have a right to associate with one another in a community of believers, or *umma*. At the same time, however, numerous verses require Muslims to show great respect to Jews, Christians, and other adherents of monotheistic faiths. These followers of monotheistic faiths are known as "People of the Book" because, according to the Koran, the founders of their religions were all Messengers bearing an episodic outpouring of revelation from one God. The Koran asserts, "Say: 'We believe in God, and that which has been sent down on us, and sent down on

Abraham and Ishmael, Isaac and Jacob, and the Tribes, and in that which was given to Moses and Jesus, and the Prophets, of their Lord; we make no division between any of them, and to Him we surrender.'" Muḥammad declared that he was "not an innovation among the Messengers." Further, the Koran teaches, according to Islam scholar Fazlur Rahman, that "all Messengers have preached essentially the same message."[12]

The Koran upholds and praises the Torah as well as the New Testament: "We gave to [Jesus] the Gospel, wherein is guidance and light, and confirming the Torah before it, as a guidance and an admonition unto the godfearing." Accordingly, Jews and Christians are highly regarded in the sight of God. In this connection, the Koran states, "Surely they that believe, and those of Jewry, and the Christians, and those Sabaeans, whoso believes in God and the Last Day, and works righteousness—their wage awaits them with their Lord, and no fear shall be on them, neither shall they sorrow." The Koran invites cooperation between Muslims, on the one hand, and Jews and Christians, on the other: "Say: 'People of the Book! Come now to a word common between us and you, that we serve none but God.'"[13]

The Koran asserts that the Christian community has a right to govern itself based on the laws of the New Testament rather than the laws of the Koran: "So let the People of the Gospel judge according to what God has sent down therein." In keeping with this and other Koranic passages, under the practice of Muḥammad as well as later Islamic jurisprudence, Christian and Jewish communities within Islamic lands were allowed to apply their own laws regarding personal status and relations.[14]

The Koran requires Muslims to respect the views even of nonbelievers who are not People of the Book. It states, "To you your religion, and to me my religion!" Some passages suggest that nonbelievers are to be moved by persuasion, not force. For example, the Koran advises us, "Help one another to piety and godfearing; do not help each other to sin and enmity." Further, we are only allowed to "remind" others, not force them into belief: "Thou art not charged to oversee them." Based on the authority of passages like these, the early Muslim community practiced significant tolerance toward Jews and Christians living in territory under its control.[15]

# The Bahá'í Faith and the Bahá'í Writings

The Bahá'í writings enjoin all of us to search independently for the truth and to exert our full capacities for human reasoning in applying spiritual principles to practical problems. They teach that religion and science should be in harmony, and that faith ought to be confirmed by reason. In the words of 'Abdu'l-Bahá, "religion and science walk hand in hand, and any religion contrary to science is not the truth." In keeping with this approach to religion and reason, the Bahá'í writings explicitly advocate freedom of religion as well as free speech. However, they advise that we be moderate and respectful in the exercise of our right to free speech. In this regard, 'Abdu'l-Bahá stated that "just as in the world of politics there is need for free thought, likewise in the world of religion there should be the right of unrestricted individual belief. . . . When freedom of conscience, liberty of thought and right of speech prevail—that is to say, when every man according to his own idealization may give expression to his beliefs—development and growth are inevitable."[16]

Furthermore, Bahá'u'lláh advocated religious concord. Bahá'u'lláh counseled, "Consort with the followers of all religions in a spirit of friendliness and fellowship." And 'Abdu'l-Bahá went so far as to proclaim, "An essential principle of Bahá'u'lláh's teaching is that religion must be the cause of unity and love amongst men; . . . Religion is not intended to arouse enmity and hatred nor to become the source of tyranny and injustice. Should it prove to be the cause of hostility, discord and the alienation of mankind, assuredly the absence of religion would be preferable."[17]

# 9

## The Status
## of Women

*Women and men have been and will always be equal in the sight of God.*

—Bahá'u'lláh

# The Status of Women in the Scriptures

Most of the scriptures contain passages that imply an inferior social status for women. Historically, men have invoked these passages to justify the subjugation of women. For this reason, many observers are skeptical about the attitude of the world's religions toward women. In this chapter I note some of these passages apparently subordinating women to men.

However, this chapter also highlights the existence of many other passages affirming the equal *spiritual* dignity of women and men. This fundamental principle of equal spiritual dignity may, in light of social conditions today, justify granting women full equality with men in the societal realm. Indeed, if we examine the scriptures chronologically (as they are presented here), we can perceive an evolution in their attitudes toward the social role of women. In particular, we can identify over time the granting of ever more expansive rights to women.

Needless to say, this very brief chapter can only provide a few examples from the scriptures of each religion. Its modest purpose is to suggest that the scriptures establish a moral basis for recognizing the equal dignity, and rights, of women and men, even if they also affirm the legitimacy of different social roles for the sexes.

# Hinduism and the
# Bhagavad Gita

The Bhagavad Gita contains only a passing reference to women. It asserts, "For if they take refuge in Me, son of Pṛthā, / Even those who may be of base origin, / Women, men of the artisan caste, and serfs too, / Even they go to the highest goal."[1] This passage seems to equate women with serfs and those of "base origin," and thus implies their social inferiority to men. But it simultaneously reaffirms the equal opportunity of all to achieve spiritual enlightenment. It articulates a principle that all of us, including women, have the same potential spiritual capacity, and therefore the same inherent dignity.

# Judaism and the
# Hebrew Scriptures

There are many passages in the Hebrew scriptures that seem to imply the inferiority of women to men. For example, the story of Genesis recounts that the first woman, Eve, was created by God to be a "fitting helper" to her husband, the first man, Adam, and that she was formed from one of his ribs. Moreover, the serpent enticed Eve to eat the fruit from the tree in the Garden of Eden whose fruit God had forbidden Adam and Eve to eat. She ate the fruit herself and also gave it to Adam. God then said he would punish Eve by making her pangs in childbearing severe; further, he commanded, "your husband . . . shall rule over you."[2]

This account of the creation of women—including its depiction of women as perpetrators of the moral downfall of men, and its command that husbands shall rule over their wives—has been used by men for millennia to justify their social domination of women. Further, on the basis of this and other stories in the Hebrew scriptures, rabbinical law discriminated against women in many ways.[3]

Nevertheless, it is possible to interpret the creation story in Genesis as affirming the equal spiritual, and even social, dignity of women and men. For Genesis also states that "God created man in His image, in the image of God He created him; male and female He created them." This passage clearly implies that men and women both are created in God's image, and therefore have an equal potential to acquire the spiritual attributes of God. Genesis further asserts that men and women are created of the same flesh; hence "a man leaves his father and mother and clings to his wife, so that they become one flesh." This particular passage's portrayal of men does not characterize them as domineering. On the contrary, it implies that men are, and should be, dependent on their wives. They are to consider themselves as united with their wives on a footing of equality, rather than as superior and therefore of a different "flesh."[4]

In addition, there are other stories in the Hebrew scriptures that dignify women. These include the account of the strong woman running her own business in chapter 31 of Proverbs. And in another chapter of Proverbs, wisdom and understanding are characterized as feminine virtues.[5] These types of passages, while relatively few in number, certainly imply that women have an equal spiritual status to that of men. They further suggest that women ought to be given more freedom than they traditionally enjoyed in earlier times, even if they were not to be treated as the full social equals of men.

# Buddhism and Buddhist Scriptures

According to Buddhist scriptures, the Buddha did not directly challenge the patriarchal traditions of society relating to the social status of women. In fact, a number of his recorded teachings appear to discriminate against women. For example, female monks had to abide by special rules that did not apply to male members of the monastic community, or *sangha*. Further, some schools of Buddhism held that women were incapable of attaining Buddhahood.[6]

On the other hand, the Buddha did eventually allow for the admission of women to an order of monks, having been persuaded to do so by his disciple Ānanda. And he affirmed the fundamental spiritual equality of men and women: "Whoever has such a vehicle, whether a woman or a man, Shall indeed, by means of that vehicle, Come to *nirvāna*." He also contravened the social attitudes of the time that looked with disfavor on the birth of a daughter by declaring that a "woman child, O Lord of men, may prove, Even a better offspring than a male." Thus, the Buddha did not overturn the patriarchal system of his time, but he did at least clearly announce the inherently equal spiritual dignity of women and men.[7]

# Confucianism and the Analects

Confucius, in keeping with the views of his age and culture, saw women as having an inferior social position to men. For example, in the Analects Confucius stated, "Women and little people are hard to handle. If you let them get close, they presume; if you keep them at a distance, they resent it." This passage equates women with "little people" and describes them as having an inherent character flaw of being "hard to handle." Moreover, in later Confucian texts and in the social practices and traditions of Confucianism women were often relegated to an inferior role.[8]

On the other hand, according to Confucius's teachings, in principle even a woman could achieve the status of "noble person," an alternative translation of "gentleman." And Confucianism scholars E. Bruce Brooks and A. Taeko Brooks more sympathetically interpret the above passage as reflecting the greater visibility of women in Confucian society and an increasing respect for personal feelings. These include "rising emotional expectations" that can engender resentment when they are frustrated. Brooks and Brooks also note that in verse 6.28 the Analects acknowledges that some women had achieved court rank. Thus, again, there may be a basis in the Analects for recognizing the fundamentally equal spiritual dignity of women and men and at least the potential for a higher social standing for women to evolve over time.[9]

# Christianity and the New Testament

There are many passages in the New Testament, especially in the writings of St. Paul and St. Peter, that suggest that women should be subservient to men. For example, St. Paul encouraged consultation among male believers, but apparently prohibited the participation of women in church discussions. St. Paul also instructed, "Wives, be subject to your husbands, as is fitting in the Lord." And St. Peter likewise counseled, "Wives, . . . accept the authority of your husbands, so that, even if some of them do not obey the word, they may be won over without a word by their wives' conduct, when they see the purity and reverence of your lives. . . . Thus Sarah obeyed Abraham and called him lord."[10]

Some scholars have regarded these and other passages as reflecting patriarchal assumptions of the era rather than immutable moral principles. Moreover, these verses must be read in the context of many others that imply the fundamental spiritual interdependence of men and women and women's essential spiritual equality with men. St. Paul suggested this interdependence and equality in affirming, "In the Lord woman is not independent of man or man independent of woman." And again he declared, "There . . . is no longer male and female; for all of you are one in Christ Jesus." Furthermore, it is noteworthy that women, including Mary Magdalene, were among those in the group surrounding Jesus. Thus, according to one contemporary interpreter, "equality of the sexes in the sight of God is reflected throughout the gospels, whether in the celebration of the birth of Christ, membership of Jesus' family of faith, or witnessing to the resurrection."[11]

# Islam and the Koran

There are several passages in the Koran that have been used by men to justify the inferior treatment of women. For example, one verse suggests that while women and men generally have equivalent rights, men have slightly more rights and obligations than women. This verse asserts, "Women have such honourable rights as obligations, but their men have a degree above them." The Koran also states, "Men are the managers of the affairs of women for that God has preferred in bounty one of them over another, and for that they have expended of their property." And the Koran's inheritance rules also favor men. These verses, and others relating to rights of husbands to divorce and sometimes discipline their wives, have been cited by many interpreters to rationalize the subjugation of women.[12]

On the other hand, when viewed in sociohistorical perspective, the Koran can be seen as rescuing women from nonpersonhood under traditional Arabic culture and as promoting their rights. In the words of legal scholar Ann Elizabeth Mayer, the Koran "devotes considerable attention to women. Qur'anic innovations tend in the direction of enhancing women's rights and elevating their status and dignity. In an environment where women were so devalued that female infanticide was a common and tolerated practice, the Qur'an introduced reforms that prohibited female infanticide, permitted women to inherit, restricted the practice of polygamy, curbed abuses of divorce by husbands, and gave women the ownership of the dower, which had previously been paid to the bride's father."[13]

According to another Western scholar, the Koran insists on "the religious and spiritual equality of men and women." For example, it states, "And whosoever does deeds of righteousness, be it male or female, believing—they shall enter Paradise." Numerous passages in the Koran, such as the one just quoted, explicitly treat men and women equally and refer to them side-by-side. To give another example, the Koran affirms, "To the men a share from what they have earned, and to the women a share from what they have earned." Furthermore, in his Farewell Sermon, Muḥammad said, "Ye people! ye have rights over your wives and your wives have rights over you."[14]

Interpreters maintaining that the Koran supports the fundamental equality of men and women point out that those verses implying that men have somewhat greater rights and obligations than women reflect the more significant social and financial responsibilities placed upon men at the time of the Koran's revelation. These interpreters also suggest that, apart from these Koranic principles, many discriminatory rules that evolved under Islamic law did not derive from the Koran, but rather from the opinions of male jurists or from patriarchal traditions.[15]

# The Bahá'í Faith and the Bahá'í Writings

The Bahá'í writings firmly uphold the spiritual equality of women and men. Bahá'u'lláh taught that "women and men have been and will always be equal in the sight of God." Moreover, the Bahá'í writings state that the social status of women must be elevated to a level of full equality with men. In this connection, 'Abdu'l-Bahá affirmed, "The world of humanity is possessed of two wings: the male and the female. So long as these two wings are not equivalent in strength, the bird will not fly. Until womankind reaches the same degree as man, until she enjoys the same arena of activity, extraordinary attainment for humanity will not be realized; . . . Therefore, woman must receive the same education as man and all inequality be adjusted." 'Abdu'l-Bahá also declared that the achievement of world peace will only be possible when women occupy positions of governmental leadership and attain complete equality with men in public affairs: "When women participate fully and equally in the affairs of the world, when they enter confidently and capably the great arena of laws and politics, war will cease."[16]

In the private sphere, the Bahá'í writings view marriage as an equal partnership and endorse the development of strong family bonds between husbands and wives, and parents and children, based on mutual respect: "The integrity of the family bond must be constantly considered, and the rights of the individual members must not be transgressed. . . . All these rights and prerogatives must be conserved, yet the unity of the family must be sustained. The injury of one shall be considered the injury of all; the comfort of each, the comfort of all; the honor of one, the honor of all."[17]

# 10

# A Trust Theory of Government and Limited State Sovereignty

*Concern yourself with what is rightful for the people.*

—Confucius

# A Trust Theory of Government and Limited Sovereignty in the Scriptures

Passages from almost all the scriptures condemn despotism and impose duties on leaders to behave fairly and with justice towards the people over whom they exercise leadership. These passages insist that leaders must act as trustees of God or some higher moral authority for the benefit of their people, and not pursue their own selfish interests. By articulating a trust theory of government, these scriptural passages implicitly recognize rights of citizens to be treated fairly by their leaders, or to what we would today refer to as civil and political human rights. Thus, the passages imply that the sovereignty of rulers or states is circumscribed by their duties to act as trustees for the benefit of their people.

# Hinduism and the Bhagavad Gita

The Bhagavad Gita does not explicitly articulate a trust theory of government or a principle of limited state sovereignty. However, many of the virtues that it praises are consistent with these principles and appear to apply to rulers as well as citizens. For example, the Gita criticizes those who take pride in being "rich," "of noble birth," or "mighty," which could include governors. It instead counsels us to pursue such virtues as "generosity," "harmlessness," "compassion towards creatures," and "no greedy desire"—virtues of rulers that are endorsed by a trust theory of government. Further, the Gita implies that all of us, including officials, are subject to "the law's injunctions" and thus are obligated to abide by moral law and ethical principles. This view is compatible with a principle of limited state sovereignty.[1]

# Judaism and the Hebrew Scriptures

The Hebrew scriptures instruct kings and officials to fulfill a number of obligations to their people. Kings must rule with justice, providing for the needs of the destitute and protecting citizens from all kinds of oppression: "O God, endow the king with Your judgments, the king's son with Your righteousness; that he may judge Your people rightly, Your lowly ones, justly. . . . Let him champion the lowly among the people, deliver the needy folk, and crush those who wrong them. . . . For he saves the needy who cry out, the lowly who have no helper. He cares about the poor and the needy; He brings the needy deliverance. He redeems them from fraud and lawlessness."[2]

The Torah makes clear that kings, like the people, must obey the law. It asserts that any Israeli king must comply with the Torah and must at all times have a copy of the Teaching with him while seated on his throne: "Let it remain with him and let him read in it all his life, so that he may learn to revere the Lord his God, to observe faithfully every word of this Teaching as well as these laws. Thus he will not act haughtily toward his fellows or deviate from the Instruction to the right or to the left, to the end that he and his descendants may reign long in the midst of Israel." As we have seen, officials must "govern the people with due justice" and must act without "partiality." And all persons must be treated as equal before the law.[3]

These passages suggest that the Hebrew scriptures adopt a practical view of the authority of civil government. Nations and governments have no moral authority by themselves and are subject to God and divine law. Thus Isaiah states of God, "He brings potentates to naught, Makes rulers of the earth as nothing." Indeed, according to one twentieth-century interpreter, "it is a striking feature of the Jewish development that the king is never deified or regarded as the representative of God. He is simply the leader of the people in war and peace. . . . The kings could not make laws; for the law came from a divine revelation." Legal scholar Shabtai Rosenne has concluded that classic "Jewish religio-legal teaching thus provides a forceful denial of the sacred egoism implicit in the notion of act of State, or Staatsräson, or Sovereignty itself."[4]

# Buddhism and Buddhist Scriptures

Buddhist scriptures recount that the Buddha laid down various prescriptions for the behavior of kings, including a universal monarch. He expected them, in the words of one scholar, to "govern justly and impartially. There are three components of the concept of righteousness: impartiality, just requital and truthfulness. While impartiality and fair play are emphasized for kings, their rule is expected to be pervaded by the spirit of benevolence. Above the social and political order was the Buddhist concept of dharma, the cosmic order in the universe, and the king had not merely to respect this order but also as the 'wheel-turning monarch' to see that this order was reflected in his regime." According to Buddhist scriptures, kings have a responsibility to uphold law and order for the safety of the people, to advance their economic welfare, and to encourage them, primarily through moral education, to treat one another humanely. Thus, one Buddhist scholar concludes that in the Buddhist view kingly power is "subservient to the rule of righteousness. . . . The state must be vigilant but human rights must not be interfered with." Further, "Ultimate sovereignty resided not in any ruler, human or divine, nor in any body governing the state nor in the state itself but in Dhamma, the eternal principles of righteousness."[5]

# Confucianism, the Analects, and the Works of Mencius

In the Analects Confucius emphasized the importance of trust in a government by the people as a cornerstone of the government's legitimacy. When asked about government, he observed, "Enough food; enough weapons; the people having confidence in [the ruler]." When asked which of these three a ruler could first sacrifice, Confucius replied weapons. Of food and trust, he said food should then be given up because "since antiquity there has always been death, but if the people lack confidence, [the ruler] cannot stand." Indeed, Confucius believed that the most important factor in judging leaders is whether or not they rule for the benefit of the people. He said that leaders must govern assiduously in good faith and must be "solicitous of others." And Confucius advised rulers: "Concern yourself with what is rightful for the people."[6]

Moreover, according to Confucius, government leaders must be moral examples to the populace: "If he cannot correct his own person, how can he be good enough to correct others?" Rulers should govern by means of virtue, for in doing so citizens will help maintain order voluntarily out of their own sense of right rather than because of fear of punishment: "Lead them with government and regulate them by punishments, and the people will evade them with no sense of shame. Lead them with virtue and regulate them by ritual, and they will acquire a sense of shame—and moreover, they will be orderly."[7]

Mencius also stressed that rulers have duties to protect citizens. He explicitly affirmed that the people, rather than the sovereign, have the highest moral worth: "'The people are the most important element *in a nation*; the spirits of the land and grain are the next; the sovereign is the lightest.'"[8]

# Christianity and the New Testament

Passages from the New Testament might be interpreted to teach that rulers have a mandate from God only when they govern with justice and thereby serve God. For example, St. Peter and the apostles responded to an allegation that they were teaching the new religion of Christianity despite commands by the authorities to stop as follows: "'We must obey God rather than any human authority.'" This statement implies that human authorities are subject to divinely-ordained principles of justice. In this connection, Jesus counseled the apostles, "You know that the rulers of the Gentiles lord it over them, and their great ones are tyrants over them. It will not be so among you; but whoever wishes to be great among you must be your servant, and whoever wishes to be first among you must be your slave; just as the Son of Man came not to be served but to serve, and to give his life a ransom for many." This statement seems to endorse a "service" conception of authority and to condemn tyranny. And according to St. Paul, in the end only God is sovereign. The authority of earthly rulers is purely contingent and temporary: "Then comes the end, when he hands over the kingdom to God the Father, after he has destroyed every ruler and every authority and power."[9]

One scholar has pointed out that the founders of the Reformation "took their starting point in the doctrine of restricted sovereignty. For the very reason that absolute sovereignty belongs to God, no one in this world, be it king or prince or pope, can be considered sovereign in an absolute way. Secular sovereignty by definition is limited. The prince is entrusted with certain powers for the benefit of his subjects and he may use these powers for that purpose only."[10]

# Islam and the Koran

The Koran asserts that God alone possesses absolute sovereignty and authority. It states that secular rulers cannot claim any "divine" right to govern, based on verses such as this: "It belongs not to any mortal that God should give him the Book, the Judgment, the Prophethood, then he should say to men, 'Be you servants to me apart from God.'" Further, "to God belongs the kingdom of the heavens and of the earth, and all that is between them." In a verse that Muslim jurists have interpreted to apply to all people, including governors, the Koran affirms, "God commands you to deliver trusts back to their owners; and when you judge between the people, that you judge with justice." The Koran also says that King David was an earthly trustee of God, and that he was obligated to rule with justice: "'David, behold, We have appointed thee a viceroy in the earth; therefore judge between men justly, and follow not caprice.'"[11]

In keeping with the emphasis in these verses on the primacy of God and divinely-revealed moral principles over secular power, a number of Koranic passages imply that the only function of a nation—including nations of Muslims, Jews, or Christians—is to promote the good and to prevent injustice. For example, the Koran counsels believers, "Let there be one nation of you, calling to good, and bidding to honour, and forbidding dishonour." The Koran further states, "Some of the People of the Book are a nation upstanding . . . bidding to honour and forbidding dishonour, vying one with the other in good works; those are of the righteous." In this connection, a hadith affirms, "The most beloved in the eyes of Allah is the just ruler and the most hateful in his eyes is the unjust ruler."[12]

Under classical Sunni law the caliph was not regarded as an absolute ruler. Instead, he was seen as God's deputy on earth. As a deputy of God, he was obligated to honor the law of God and carry out justice. According to religion scholar Majid Khadduri, the "caliph's powers were derived from and limited by the divine law; only his appointment was made by the people." Another scholar has noted that, in theory, "the people could impeach the caliph if he failed to perform his functions according to his trust."[13]

# The Bahá'í Faith and the Bahá'í Writings

Bahá'u'lláh exhorted monarchs and rulers to treat their subjects justly and with concern for their well-being: "We cherish the hope that the light of justice may shine upon the world and sanctify it from tyranny. If the rulers and kings of the earth, the symbols of the power of God, exalted be His glory, arise and resolve to dedicate themselves to whatever will promote the highest interests of the whole of humanity, the reign of justice will assuredly be established amongst the children of men, and the effulgence of its light will envelop the whole earth." Bahá'u'lláh made the same appeal to elected government leaders: "O ye the elected representatives of the people in every land! Take ye counsel together, and let your concern be only for that which profiteth mankind and bettereth the condition thereof."[14]

Bahá'u'lláh enjoined rulers to cease spending on armaments, devote their resources to the welfare of their people, and treat citizens as they themselves would wish to be treated. He urged them to honor their duty to protect human rights and to succor the oppressed: "For is it not your clear duty to restrain the tyranny of the oppressor, and to deal equitably with your subjects, that your high sense of justice may be fully demonstrated to all mankind? God hath committed into your hands the reins of the government of the people, that ye may rule with justice over them, safeguard the rights of the downtrodden, and punish the wrongdoers." 'Abdu'l-Bahá affirmed that governments must ensure "the free exercise of the individual's rights, and the security of his person and property."[15]

In keeping with these teachings on human rights and on government as a sacred trust, the Bahá'í writings reject an extreme doctrine of state sovereignty. Shoghi Effendi asserted, "The anarchy inherent in state sovereignty is moving towards a climax. A world, growing to maturity, must abandon this fetish, recognize the oneness and wholeness of human relationships, and establish once for all the machinery that can best incarnate this fundamental principle of its life."[16]

# 11

# Open-Minded Consultation

*Take ye counsel together in all matters, inasmuch as consultation is the lamp of guidance which leadeth the way, and is the bestower of understanding.*

—Bahá'u'lláh

# Open-Minded Consultation in the Scriptures

Most of the scriptures contain passages that promote frank and open-minded consultation among individuals or leaders as a method of exploring the truth or solving problems in light of ethical principles. They imply that "consultation" in this ethical sense does not mean mere discussion or debate. Rather, it signifies an open-minded search for the best answer to a problem that draws upon the unique perspective and wisdom that each participant can provide. Accordingly, as participants, we should engage in consultation with an attitude of humility and respect for the views of others, and a willingness to see the merit in their opinions and to revise our own views accordingly. Indeed, many passages in scriptures suggest that in consultation we should actively seek out the views of others and realize that others may perceive an angle of the truth that we fail to apprehend.

Perhaps most importantly, the passages imply that consultation proceeds from an attitude that a solution can be arrived at harmoniously, even though our views are freely expressed and may well appear at first to conflict with those of others. The ultimate desired outcome of this exchange of differing views is harmony of opinion, if possible, rather than simply the mechanical production of a numerical majority vote in favor of a particular course of action, even if the consultation is followed by some kind of voting procedure.

# Hinduism and the Bhagavad Gita

The Bhagavad Gita, while not explicitly referring to consultation, nevertheless condemns "harshness (of speech)" and "backbiting."[1] It therefore implies that we should converse with one another respectfully, directly, and with open minds. Moreover, the Gita itself is structured as a discourse between Arjuna and Krishna, suggesting that spiritual truth can best be ascertained through consultation and dialogue.

# Judaism and the Hebrew Scriptures

An ethical principle of consultation is found in the Hebrew scriptures. For example, the Torah affirms that magistrates should "not be partial in judgment," but rather "hear out low and high alike." A verse in Proverbs declares that "plans are foiled for want of counsel, But they succeed through many advisers." Kings are wisely to consider various points of view: "Koheleth . . . listened to and tested the soundness of many maxims." Similarly, we should consult with one another with a view to speaking, and ascertaining, the truth and implementing justice: "These are the things you are to do: Speak the truth to one another, render true and perfect justice in your gates." Philosopher Lenn E. Goodman observes that in light of Genesis' language of "Let us make man in our image, after our likeness" the rabbis "remark that even God commences nothing without consultation." The principle of consultation also found expression in Talmudic dialogue among rabbis and scholars. And the Talmud required the consent of the council of rabbis before the commencement of an optional war. It also required judges to consult with one another while freely expressing their own opinions.[2]

# Buddhism and Buddhist Scriptures

Buddhist scriptures indicate that the Buddha called on us to be open to other perspectives. According to one scholar, we should give others the benefit of the doubt when we converse with them and accept "all [we] honestly can of the other's position." The Buddha counseled monks not to "be afraid of others' views." He opposed religious dissension and arguments based on exclusive claims to know the truth. We should engage in dialogue with the desire to search for truth and without discord: "Speak the truth; do not yield to anger." Through the parable of the blind men and the elephant, the Buddha taught that truth has many angles. In the parable, a group of blind men gather around an elephant and, after feeling different parts of it with their hands, argue about what it is and what its qualities are. Those touching the head think it is like a pot; those touching the ear think it is like a winnowing basket; those touching the tusk think it is like a plowshare; and those touching the trunk think it is like a plow. The Buddha thus implied that we can only perceive the full richness of truth through open-minded consultation rather than quarreling or clinging to our own narrow perspective.[3]

# Confucianism, the Analects, and the Works of Mencius

According to the Analects, we should humbly consult with others. Moreover, we should learn from others, both by observing their admirable behavior and seeking to emulate it, and by observing their wrongful conduct and seeking to avoid it: "When he sees a worthy man, let him think how he might come up to him; when he sees an unworthy man, let him examine within himself."[4]

Confucius further asserted, "When I am walking in a group of three people, there will surely be a teacher for me among them. I pick out the good parts and follow them; the bad parts, and change them." We should take advantage of opportunities to consult with others who are willing to do so: "If he can be talked to and you do not talk to him, you waste the man." Confucius implied that we should examine our own views and shortcomings with a critical eye rather than attacking the perspectives and failings of others. On the other hand, we should not reflexively follow the views of others simply to be accepted: "The gentleman is harmonious but not conformist. The little man is conformist but not harmonious." Indeed, Confucius taught that we should not blindly follow popular opinion: "When the many hate him, one must always look into it; when the many love him, one must always look into it."[5]

Consistent with these sayings of Confucius, Mencius later counseled rulers to consult with their people and carefully consider their views in making any important decision. These included decisions concerning the appointment or dismissal of officials and the imposition of capital punishment. Mencius taught further that even if the people were in accord on an issue, a ruler should not unthinkingly follow their will. Instead, he should investigate and confirm the correctness or moral propriety of their views, and then he should make his decision and take appropriate action. This procedure would help prevent unjust oppression based on majority opinion.[6]

# Christianity and the New Testament

A number of New Testament passages counsel Christian believers to practice open-minded consultation. In this process each person expresses his own views, in his unique way, while considering thoughtfully the views of others and seeking to learn from them. St. Paul stated in his first letter to the Corinthians, "When you come together, each one has a hymn, a lesson, a revelation, a tongue, or an interpretation. . . . Let two or three prophets speak, and let the others weigh what is said. If a revelation is made to someone else sitting nearby, let the first person be silent. For you can all prophesy one by one, so that all may learn and all be encouraged." Jesus's disciples also consulted with one another, for example, about the continuing validity of the Mosaic law of circumcision. Theologian John H. Yoder has affirmed with respect to the concept of consultation: "As is said most simply in Paul's epistle to the Corinthians, the right way for believers to hold a meeting in the power of the Holy Spirit is to authorize everyone to speak."[7]

# Islam and the Koran

Various verses of the Koran similarly support open-minded consultation, referred to as *shūrā*. For example, the Koran asserts, "Take counsel with them in the affair; and when thou art resolved, put thy trust in God." A hadith endorses the existence of differences of opinion as part of the process of investigating the truth. According to Muḥammad, "'If there is a difference of opinion within my community that is a sign of the bounty of Allah.'" Another hadith recounts that Muḥammad answered a question about how the believers should resolve a problem after his death if he or the Koran had not explicitly dealt with it as follows: "'Get together amongst my followers and place the matter before them for consultation. Do not make decisions on the opinions of any single person.'" Many traditions indicate that Muḥammad consulted with his followers as a regular practice. He would honor a decision arrived at by the majority of them even if the decision did not agree with his own views. He would only refuse to accept the decision if it contravened the injunctions of the Koran.[8]

Many contemporary scholars, including Muslims, have argued that by virtue of these Koranic verses and hadiths, Islam requires open-minded consultation between leaders and their people. For example, according to C. G. Weeramantry, a governor "has a duty to consult and draw his subjects into a democratic participation in the processes of government." Riffat Hassan likewise affirms that because "the principle of mutual consultation ("shurā") . . . is mandatory . . . , it is a Muslim's fundamental right to participate in as many aspects of the community's life as possible."[9]

# The Bahá'í Faith and the Bahá'í Writings

The Bahá'í writings encourage all of us, and all social institutions, to practice open-minded consultation. Bahá'u'lláh declared,

"Take ye counsel together in all matters, inasmuch as consultation is the lamp of guidance which leadeth the way, and is the bestower of understanding." In the Bahá'í view, as participants in consultation, we must freely express our views, even if these views initially clash with those of others. But we must do so with the ultimate purpose of reaching agreement and with detachment from our own opinions. 'Abdu'l-Bahá explained the process of open-minded consultation as follows:

Consultation must have for its object the investigation of truth. He who expresses an opinion should not voice it as correct and right but set it forth as a contribution to the consensus of opinion, for the light of reality becomes apparent when two opinions coincide. . . . Before expressing his own views he should carefully consider the views already advanced by others. If he finds that a previously expressed opinion is more true and worthy, he should accept it immediately and not willfully hold to an opinion of his own. By this excellent method he endeavors to arrive at unity and truth. . . . The most memorable instance of spiritual consultation was the meeting of the disciples of Jesus Christ upon the mount after His ascension. . . . This was true consultation.[10]

# 12

# Respect for Governments and Law

*O believers, obey God, and obey the Messenger and those in authority among you.*

—The Koran

# Respect for Governments and Law in the Scriptures

Passages from all the scriptures enjoin us to obey the law and those in authority in the interest of maintaining civil order and peace. However, as we saw in chapter 10, according to these passages, political leaders and institutions are not given absolute divine sanction. The scriptures consequently also recognize that we may have a right not to obey a governmental order that requires us directly to contravene fundamental moral duties. Some passages allow rebellion against tyranny as an absolute last resort. Many of the scriptures also endorse long-term reforms of the character and behavior of political institutions, rulers, and individuals so that they implement the moral teachings prescribed by the scriptures.

# Hinduism and the Bhagavad Gita

The Bhagavad Gita teaches that those who are tempted by vices must conform their actions with the law: "Whoso neglects the law's injunction, / And lives according to his own wilful desires, / He does not attain perfection, / Nor bliss, nor the highest goal. Therefore let the law be thy authority / In determining what should and should not be done. Knowing (action) laid down in the law's in-

junctions, / Thou shouldst do (such) action in this world." Despite
this principle of respect for law, some modern interpreters of the
Gita have found, in Arjuna's questioning of his duty to fight, the
moral authority for an individual to refuse to follow any unreasonable demands of societal authorities.[1]

# Judaism and the Hebrew Scriptures

The Hebrew scriptures counsel Jews to respect government and
to promote the interests of the city in which they reside: "Seek the
welfare of the city to which I [God] have exiled you and pray to the
Lord in its behalf." Moreover, Ecclesiastes contains the pragmatic
injunction to "'obey the king's orders—and don't rush into utter-
ing an oath by God.'. . . One who obeys orders will not suffer from
the dangerous situation." Further, we must obey decisions of priests
or magistrates as a matter of moral obligation: "You shall act in
accordance with the instructions given you and the ruling handed
down to you; you must not deviate from the verdict that they announce to you either to the right or to the left."[2]

These practical and moral counsels of obedience to kings and
magistrates do not mean that those in authority should *always* be
obeyed. The Hebrew scriptures provide examples of disobedience
to kings when required by moral principle, such as the refusal of
Hebrew midwives to obey Pharaoh's order to kill all Hebrew new-
born boys. Subsequent commentaries by rabbis ruled that nonviolent resistance is justified if the fundamentals of religious belief are
at stake. For example, Maimonides, the prominent twelfth-century
rabbinical scholar, affirmed that while rebels can be punished by

death, no liability is incurred for disobeying a royal decree as a result of performing a religious command "because (when there is a conflict) between the edict of the Master (God) and the edict of the servant (the king), the former takes precedence of the latter." According to one contemporary theologian, "many instances could be cited of disobedience to established authority, whether Jewish or non-Jewish, where such authority violated the basic moral and religious convictions of Judaism."[3]

# Buddhism and Buddhist Scriptures

Buddhist scriptures in general counsel obedience to government but approve of revolution against oppressive rulers in extreme cases. According to one contemporary Buddhist scholar, "Our allegiance to a law-making body is always qualified and the unjust legislation of such body need not justify obedience." The Buddha thus advised monks to follow a king's or a state's orders only if they were not "morally repugnant." Nevertheless, even when a right of rebellion exists, Buddhist texts indicate that nonviolent resistance is always morally superior to the use of force.[4]

# Confucianism, the Analects, and the Works of Mencius

In the Analects, Confucius taught the principle of respect for rulers. Confucius also asserted that laws are necessary and that citi-

zens bear individual responsibility for obeying just laws. He re-
marked, "The gentleman likes justice; the little man likes mercy."
But Confucius also allowed for, and indeed encouraged, criticism
of governments that were not practicing humaneness. He stated
with respect to a ruler: "If he is good and no one disobeys, is that
not good? But if he is *not* good and no one disobeys, would this not
be one saying that could destroy a state?" (The popular saying to
which Confucius was referring is: "I have no joy in being a ruler
save in being able to speak and have no one disobey.") Although
Confucius exhorted citizens and ministers generally to obey a moral
ruler, when obedience would transgress the principle of humaneness he then counseled passive disobedience: "Those whom one
calls great ministers serve their ruler according to the Way, and when
they can do so no longer, they stop."[5]

Later Confucian writings, especially those of Mencius, recognize that people may revolt against tyranny as an absolute last resort, after they have pleaded with the tyrant numerous times.
Mencius exhorted individuals to resist peacefully a tyrannical governor. But he also recognized that tyranny might provoke rebellion, which in his view was, according to one scholar, "a last desperate recourse for an exasperated people, understandable but not to
be commended." Mencius advised in one passage that high ministers who are relatives of a prince with egregious shortcomings should
first "remonstrate with him," and that if the prince does not "listen
to them after they have done so again and again, they ought to
dethrone him." These suggestions of the permissibility of opposing rulers in extreme circumstances indicate that in Confucianism
there was "a kind of fundamental right, albeit a right of last resort,
of the people against the ruler. Chinese rulers, however much they
might wish to, could never quite forget this claim."[6]

# Christianity and the New Testament

The New Testament advises us, in general, to obey secular authorities. When the disciples of the Pharisees asked Jesus, "Is it lawful to pay taxes to the emperor, or not?," Jesus answered, "Give therefore to the emperor the things that are the emperor's, and to God the things that are God's."[7] His statement indicates that we owe some deference to civil authority, but it does not answer the question of how much deference. In St. Paul's letter to the Romans he articulated a justification for obedience to earthly rulers that appears to elevate obedience to the status of a moral duty, because kings are the servants of God on earth:

> Let every person be subject to the governing authorities; for there is no authority except from God, and those authorities that exist have been instituted by God. Therefore whoever resists authority resists what God has appointed, and those who resist will incur judgment. For rulers are not a terror to good conduct, but to bad. Do you wish to have no fear of the authority? Then do what is good, and you will receive its approval; for it is God's servant for your good. But if you do what is wrong, you should be afraid, for the authority does not bear the sword in vain![8]

Historically, this statement led Anglicans and Lutherans to adopt a position of "'passive obedience,' according to which Christian subjects could not legitimately challenge their rulers, much less rebel against them."[9]

At the same time, other passages from the New Testament imply that moral duties may justify limited disobedience to sovereign commands. Thus, as noted earlier, when St. Peter and the apostles were accused of teaching Christianity in spite of commands not to do so, they affirmed, "We must obey God rather than any human authority." Jesus himself admonished the scribes and the Pharisees, labeling them "hypocrites" and criticizing them for having "neglected the weightier matters of the law: justice and mercy and faith." Indeed, based on these types of examples from scripture, Christian theologian Hans Küng suggests that the "Gospel sources make it abundantly clear how very much Jesus of Nazareth was a thoroughly aggressive critic of the hierarchs and court theologians and how in his case, selflessness and self-awareness, humility and toughness, gentleness and aggression belong together."[10]

Even with respect to the above statement of St. Paul from Romans that appears to adopt a rather stringent doctrine of obedience to civil authorities, there seems to be an underlying assumption that the authorities in fact require morally praiseworthy conduct and forbid morally reprehensible conduct. This passage's counsel of obedience may apply only when rulers actually govern justly and thus may implicitly justify disobedience when they do not. Nevertheless, taken as a whole these scriptural passages indicate that the "freedom of the Christian individual is . . . not to be equated with the overturning of the established social order or with arbitrary and amoral assertions of the individual's desires."[11]

# Islam and the Koran

The Koran advises us to obey secular authorities as well as God and His Prophet in this verse: "O believers, obey God, and obey the Messenger and those in authority among you. If you should quarrel on anything, refer it to God and the Messenger, if you believe in God and the Last Day; that is better, and fairer in the issue."[12] This passage appears to advise Muslims to obey authorities (whether religious or secular) *and* Muḥammad and the Koran where possible. It also suggests that in case of disputes Koranic authority and the words and example of the Prophet ought to prevail.

Under Islamic law obedience to government was viewed as necessary to assist governments in fulfilling their duty to promote justice. In this connection, according to a hadith, Muḥammad counseled obedience even to a tyrant: "If the ruler is a tyrant, he will get his punishment and you ought to have patience." So deep-rooted was this principle of obedience to government that later Muslim jurists ruled that Muslims living in a territory ruled by non-Muslims had the duty to obey the laws of the non-Muslim government.[13]

On the other hand, various verses of the Koran and certain hadiths may support rebellion as a last resort where a despotic government violates its duty to promote justice. For example, the Koran states that if a believer is "insolent against" another, the Muslim community should "fight the insolent one till it reverts to God's commandment." Another verse of the Koran asserts, "So fear you God, and obey you me, and obey not the commandment of the prodigal who do corruption in the earth, and set not things aright." And a hadith reports that Muḥammad said, "If people see an oppressor and they do not hinder him, then God will punish all of them."[14]

# The Bahá'í Faith and the Bahá'í Writings

The Bahá'í writings instruct Bahá'ís to obey the governments of the territories in which they live. They also forbid Bahá'ís from participating in partisan politics because doing so creates discord rather than concord. Bahá'u'lláh declared that Bahá'ís residing in a country "must behave towards the government of that country with loyalty, honesty and truthfulness." At the same time, the Bahá'í writings encourage Bahá'ís to strive to implement their teachings and share them with others. Moreover, Bahá'ís can resist governmental demands to recant their faith.[15]

The Bahá'í writings prohibit sedition and other forms of civil discord. For example, 'Abdu'l-Bahá explained that Bahá'u'lláh had summoned kings and rulers to international peace and unity, "that strife, warfare and sedition should pass away."[16]

# 13

## Peace, Justice, and Respect for Treaties and International Law

*The work of righteousness shall be peace, And the effect of righteousness, calm and confidence forever.*

—Isaiah 32:17

# The Duty to Promote Peace

In keeping with the scriptures' teaching that all of us have an ethical duty to act peacefully and nonviolently toward other individuals, passages from many of the scriptures endorse the cultivation of peace and cooperation among countries and other social groups. These passages further suggest that government leaders have a strong moral obligation to work diligently to achieve peace among nations and peoples.

For example, we have seen that the Bhagavad Gita teaches the virtues of nonviolence and harmlessness. The many kings of ancient India were all considered to be subject to dharma and therefore bound to observe a general principle of nonviolence. The principle of nonviolence found expression in the "Code of Manu," which was written around 100 BCE. The Code of Manu advised rulers to use conciliation to resolve their differences and to refrain from the use of force, war being permissible only as a last resort.[1]

There are passages from the Hebrew scriptures that criticize unjust wars and advocate peace among rulers. For example, King David reported that God refused to allow him to build a resting place for the Ark of the Covenant because God said to him "'you are a man of battles and have shed blood'"—an apparent reference to war being looked upon with disfavor.[2]

According to Buddhist scriptures, the Buddha urged us to dedicate our lives to peace, as reflected in his precept that we should refrain from killings others. He emphasized the "futility of warfare" and prohibited the profession of arms selling. The Buddha instructed rulers not to "foster hostility towards neighbouring kings." And he advised them: "Cultivate ties of friendship with neighbouring kings, O mighty lord, for other peoples honour kings who are steadfast in friendship."[3]

Confucius's teachings of nonviolence, noncompetition, harmony, and forgiveness between individuals provide a basis for recognizing a moral principle favoring peace among rulers and nations as well. Nevertheless, he believed that some wars were legitimate, but he maintained that these wars must be conducted ethically, by soldiers trained extensively in moral virtues. He said, "When good men have taught the people for seven years, one may then have recourse to arms."[4]

Peace between individuals is a foundational teaching of Jesus in the New Testament. This individual ethic can be understood to support an ethic of peace among nations and religious groups as well. For example, St. Paul, speaking of relations between Jews and Gentiles, wrote, "[In Jesus's] flesh he has made both groups into one and has broken down the dividing wall, that is, the hostility between us. He has abolished the law with its commandments and ordinances, that he might create in himself one new humanity in place of the two, thus making peace, and might reconcile both groups to God in one body through the cross, thus putting to death that hostility through it. So he came and proclaimed peace to you who were far off and peace to those who were near."[5]

As we saw in chapter 2, the Koran affirms that God created nations and peoples so that they could cooperate with one another, not fight: "O mankind, We have created you male and female, and appointed you races and tribes, that you may know one another." Further, the Koran calls for a "friendly" competition among nations and peoples to perform good deeds: "If God had willed, He would have made you one nation; but that He may try you in what has come to you. So be you forward in good works."[6]

Bahá'u'lláh called upon leaders to settle their disputes peacefully and without resort to war: "Beware lest ye shed the blood of anyone." Bahá'u'lláh specifically abolished the Islamic law authorizing the waging of "holy war." At the same time, he exhorted governments to implement a collective security system to preserve peace and deter aggression by states against one another.[7]

# The Close Interrelationship between Peace and Justice

Passages from all the scriptures advocate a vision of peace that includes the pursuit of justice. The scriptures imply accordingly that the use of force may sometimes be necessary to achieve justice, which in turn is seen as a requirement for a lasting peace.

For example, the Bhagavad Gita endorses the virtues of both "harmlessness" and "uprightness." It also suggests that although harmlessness and gentleness are admirable virtues, on occasion we may have a duty to use force.[8]

Many scholars of Judaism have asserted that the Hebrew scriptures are not absolutely pacifist. For example, one scholar has written, "Peace was a thing to be aimed at in the relations of the nations, but it must be established on righteousness and justice." It is a common Jewish view that the "peace expressed by shalom encompasses far more than the absence of war. Shalom means wholeness, righteousness, justice, grace, and truth. Certainly the modern theological concept that peace is not possible without justice is based on the Hebrew Scriptures." Isaiah explained this dynamic interrelationship between peace and justice: "The work of righteousness shall be peace, And the effect of righteousness, calm and confidence forever."[9]

Buddhist scriptures suggest that lasting peace requires justice and that there are times when the realization of justice may require some form of military action: "All warfare in which man tries to slay his brother is lamentable, but [the Buddha] does not teach that those who go to war in a righteous cause after having exhausted all means to preserve the peace are blameworthy. He must be blamed who is the cause of war." Similarly, as we have seen, Confucius stated in the Analects that we should not respond to malice with kindness, but rather with "uprightness." We should show kindness only in response to kindness.[10] This implies that "uprightness" (justice) sometimes must take precedence over kindness (and peace) in order to preserve the moral distinctness of kindness. This again demonstrates an interdependent relationship between justice and peace.

The New Testament's teachings manifest a multidimensional conception of peace that incorporates justice in addition to the absence of conflict. In the words of one scholar, in "the New Testament peace was still well-being and security, but the physical characteristics disappeared. The Kingdom of God consisted not in food and drink but in righteousness and peace. . . . The Christian peace was creative and dynamic." Although Jesus advocated peaceful relations among individuals, he also criticized the scribes and the Pharisees for ignoring "the weightier matters of the law: justice and mercy and faith."[11] He thus implied the interdependence of peace, justice, mercy, and faith.

The Koran also draws an interdependent linkage between peace and justice. This linkage is especially apparent in its advocacy of the concept of collective security, which is discussed in the next chapter. For example, the Koran states that "if two parties of the believers fight, put things right between them; then, if one of them is insolent against the other, fight the insolent one till it reverts to God's commandment. If it reverts, set things right between them equitably, and be just." This verse implies that force may sometimes be necessary as a last resort to restore a just peace and that a just settlement between believers can pave the way for a lasting peace. Thus, in the words of one interpreter, "Peace is an outcome of a society in which there is concern for justice and not just the absence of conflict."[12]

There also appears to be an intimate relationship in the Bahá'í conception between peace and justice. True peace can only be founded on justice for every individual, group, and nation. In the words of 'Abdu'l-Bahá, "it is time for the promulgation of universal peace—a peace based on righteousness and justice—that mankind may not be exposed to further dangers in the future."[13]

# The Duty to Respect Treaties

Passages from a number of the scriptures explicitly uphold a duty to respect treaties in relations among nations or states. They do so based on the universal moral principle that we should fulfill our promises—a principle found in all of the scriptures, as we saw in chapter 4. According to these passages, faithfulness to treaty commitments is a moral obligation and not merely a legal, social, or political one.

For example, there is evidence in the Hebrew scriptures of a strong principle of respect for treaties with foreign nations, such as the story of the Gibeonites recounted in the Book of Joshua. According to the story, the residents of Gibeon, who were afraid that Joshua would kill them if he knew they resided among the Israelites, devised a cunning plot to protect themselves. They went to Joshua and lied to him, affirming that they came from a distant land. And they proposed to make a peace treaty with him on this basis. Joshua, unaware of their deception, agreed. He "made a pact with them to spare their lives, and the chieftains of the community gave them their oath." Three days later, the Israelites learned that the Gibeonites were their neighbors and had deceived Joshua. They confronted the Gibeonites and wanted to attack them, but their chieftains stopped them, affirming, "We swore to them by the Lord, the God of Israel; therefore we cannot touch them." Law professor Michael J. Broyde points out that Jewish commentators are in agreement, in part because of the story of the Gibeonites, that "treaties are basically binding according to Jewish law."[14]

The Koran also explicitly requires treaties to be honored. It does so even with respect to treaties between Muslims and non-Muslims, except when non-Muslims violate a treaty and attack Muslims. It declares, "With them fulfil your covenant till their term." It implies that more powerful nations must not take advantage of their influence to violate their treaty commitments, and that treaties obligate powerful and weak nations equally. The Koran states, "Fulfil God's covenant, when you make covenant, and break not the oaths after they have been confirmed, and you have made God your surety; surely God knows the things you do. And be not as a woman who breaks her thread, after it is firmly spun, into fibres, by taking your oaths as mere mutual deceit, one nation being more numerous than another nation." The Koranic injunction to fulfill promises has been regarded by some scholars as consistent with, if not one of the precursors of, the international law principle that "treaties are to be observed."[15]

The Bahá'í writings condemn the violation of treaty commitments, declaring, "How often it happens that the diplomacy of nations makes a treaty of peace one day and on the morrow a declaration of war!" Further, as discussed in the next chapter, the Bahá'í writings endorse the adoption of a comprehensive collective security treaty, which would provide for strong sanctions against states that violate its provisions.[16] This teaching again emphasizes the moral imperative of observing treaty obligations.

# The Duty to Promote International Law and Cooperation

Passages from many of the scriptures imply that rulers and nations ought to adopt and abide by a common law to regulate their relationships and maintain peace among them. For example, in the Hebrew scriptures the prophet Micah foresaw a future in which nations would no longer make war and would follow a shared law: "For instruction shall come forth from Zion, The word of the Lord from Jerusalem. Thus He will judge among the many peoples, And arbitrate for the multitude of nations, However distant; And they shall beat their swords into plowshares And their spears into pruning hooks. Nation shall not take up Sword against nation; They shall never again know war." International legal historian Arthur Nussbaum has called Isaiah's version of this prophecy, which is substantially the same as Micah's, the "most important contribution of the Jewish people to the history of international law" and "a main root of modern pacifism." And according to biblical scholar Robert Gordis, Micah's vision conveys the notion of a "binding international law" and a "world government" voluntarily accepted by nations. This vision, he says, is "a far-sighted interpretation of nationalism, in which love of one's own people and loyalty to humanity represent two concentric circles."[17]

Buddhist scriptures envision that in the future a world statesman will be selected who will govern righteously, "promoting both material and spiritual welfare on the principle of the equality of man." He is obligated to provide care and protection to all citizens, especially the aged and sick; to ensure freedom of religion; to eliminate crime; and to guarantee citizens a minimal standard of economic wealth. He also must act "in consultation with enlightened religious teachers and philosophers in determining policy." However, this global ruler will achieve his status by the voluntary desire of other rulers to emulate his model state, rather than by the use of force or other forms of compulsion.[18]

Although the New Testament focuses on ethical principles applying to individuals as opposed to nations, the general ethic of peace and justice that Jesus's teachings promote is consistent with the encouragement of cooperation among nations and the development of a just law of nations. Further, in St. Paul's speech to the Athenians, referred to in chapter 8, he articulated a vision of diverse nations created by one God living in harmony with one another and together searching for God.[19]

The Koran advocates arbitration of disputes between individuals, and presumably nations, as evidenced in part by this verse: "O believers, obey God, and obey the Messenger and those in authority among you. If you should quarrel on anything, refer it to God and the Messenger, if you believe in God and the Last Day; that is better, and fairer in the issue." The passage from the Koran quoted several pages earlier (see Koran 49:9) on the resolution of disputes between believers also indicates a preference for arbitration. In keeping with these verses, Muḥammad and the early believers frequently engaged in conciliation and arbitration.[20] These passages could be read to support the practice of international arbitration.

The Bahá'í writings generally support the development of international law and cooperation. More specifically, they call for the formation of a global federation through a multilateral treaty voluntarily entered into by states. In this federation "the autonomy of its state members and the personal freedom and initiative of the individuals that compose them" would be "definitely and completely safeguarded." Among the organs of the federation would be an international tribunal, a global legislature elected through democratic procedures, and a world executive.[21]

# 14

## The Legitimate
## Use of Force

*All warfare in which man tries to slay his brother is lamentable, but [the Buddha] does not teach that those who go to war in a righteous cause after having exhausted all means to preserve the peace are blameworthy. He must be blamed who is the cause of war.*

—The Buddha

# The Legitimate Use of Force in the Scriptures

As we have seen, passages from all the scriptures endorse peaceful methods of dispute resolution between individuals, groups, rulers, and states. But other passages also reluctantly endorse the limited use of force. These passages authorize the use of force, however, only as a last resort and only to protect community members or communities from aggression or tyranny, or achieve other goals demanded by justice. In this chapter I review these passages from each religion's scriptures on legitimate reasons for the use of force. I then discuss passages from relevant scriptures relating to collective military action and to humanitarian limitations on the conduct of war.

# Hinduism and the Bhagavad Gita

The Bhagavad Gita includes many passages prescribing nonviolence and harmlessness in relations among individuals and peoples. At the same time, the discourse between Krishna and Arjuna in the

Gita takes place against the backdrop of a conflict between Arjuna and an army, some of whose members are Arjuna's friends and relatives. In the course of the dialogue Krishna urges Arjuna to do battle, which is his duty because he is a member of the warrior caste. Krishna explains that Arjuna must fulfill this duty no matter what the material consequences of doing so, emphasizing that Arjuna's soul cannot be destroyed: "Therefore fight, son of Bharata!" Passages such as this have been used by some Hindus, including Gandhi's assassin, to justify political violence. [1]

This fundamental tension in the Gita must be recognized, although scholars such as Franklin Edgerton believe it can be understood in part as a product of the text's poetic origins. And Gandhi interpreted the Gita and its battle setting as an allegory for our inner spiritual battle between good and evil. Moreover, although the literary context for the Gita is a battle, Krishna's discourses within the Gita often stress the virtues of nonviolence. Further, the Gita condemns those who take pride in slaying others. At the same time, the notion that there may be a duty to engage in battle suggests that on occasion some use of force may be necessary to maintain social order or secure justice. But the Gita implies that such force must be employed impartially and without personal animosity. One Hindu scholar attempts to integrate and summarize the Gita's teachings on nonviolence in this way: a man "'must make every effort to win over evil by peaceful means. But if that fails, he will have to fight evil with every weapon in his power. But his motive must be crystal clear. There should be no malice and hatred, no passion and selfishness, behind his actions.'"[2]

# Judaism and the Hebrew Scriptures

We have seen that a number of verses in the Hebrew scriptures promote peace. Various contemporary Jewish scholars have emphasized these kinds of passages in concluding that Judaism is fundamentally pacifist and nonviolent. However, the Hebrew scriptures do endorse war in certain cases. They state that there is a "time for war and a time for peace." Further, the Torah contains many instructions to the Israelites to wage war against the seven nearby Canaanite nations and against the Amalekites. Rabbis viewed these wars as obligatory because these nations and peoples were considered to be enemies of the Israelites. Wars in defense of the Israelites against an attack were also considered obligatory. Maimonides held, however, that the justification for nationalistic wars against the seven nations disappeared when these rival nations ceased to exist.[3]

The Torah classified other wars, such as wars of territorial expansion against distant towns, as "optional." A significant barrier to the conduct of optional wars was posed by Maimonides' requirement that the seventy-one-member council of rabbis, or Sanhedrin, consent to an optional war in order for it to be lawful. In the case of optional wars, Jewish soldiers were permitted, if an offer of peace made to a town was refused, to lay siege to the town, kill all its male inhabitants, and take as "booty the women, the children, the livestock, and everything in the town." But they were not authorized to kill women or children. The international legal jurist L. Oppenheim viewed these rules as "in no way exceptionally cruel, if looked upon from the standpoint of their time and surroundings" and as "comparatively mild."[4]

Further, the Torah suggests that war can only be waged as a last resort, after peaceful methods of dispute resolution have been exhausted. It states, "When you approach a town to attack it, you shall offer it terms of peace." In the Torah such an offer was only required in the case of optional wars against distant towns. Nevertheless, Maimonides required that an offer of peace be made even in the case of obligatory wars against the seven surrounding Canaanite nations or against the Amalekites. According to Maimonides, a defeated party's acceptance of any offer of peace must include agreement to respect the seven Noachide laws. And "once they make peace and take upon themselves the seven commandments, it is forbidden to deceive them and prove false to the covenant made with them."[5]

# Buddhism and Buddhist Scriptures

According to Buddhist scriptures, the Buddha stressed the virtues of peace among individuals and among kings. But he also authorized defensive wars and wars that are required to implement justice if all peaceful methods of bringing about justice have been tried and have failed. The Buddha stated, as already noted: "All warfare in which man tries to slay his brother is lamentable, but [the Buddha] does not teach that those who go to war in a righteous cause after having exhausted all means to preserve the peace are blameworthy. He must be blamed who is the cause of war." This passage indicates that the use of force may be allowed as a last resort in self-defense or to rectify gross injustices, but it also indicates that nonviolent methods of conflict resolution are clearly preferable. Thus, according to one scholar, the Buddha's social teaching is "not an absolute pacifism, but a philosophical ethic, making for peace, moderation, and magnanimity."[6]

# Confucianism, the Analects, and the Works of Mencius

We have seen that Confucius endorsed nonviolence as meritorious in relations between individuals. He also believed that soldiers must acquire virtues. Indeed, he suggested that no citizen be permitted to "have recourse to arms" unless he had received moral education for seven years. Later followers of Confucius also supported a general principle of nonviolence and condemned the wars that occurred among feudal states during the "Spring and Autumn" period. For example, Mencius stated, "There are men who say—'I am skilful at marshalling troops, I am skilful at conducting a battle!'—They are great criminals." He also asserted that in "the 'Spring and Autumn' there are no righteous wars." He said, nevertheless, that "instances indeed there are of one war better than another." But he affirmed that wars engaged in by hostile states could not be considered "corrective" (which could be interpreted as "righteous") because "'correction' is when the supreme authority punishes its subjects by force of arms. Hostile States do not correct one another." Confucian writings did, however, permit the use of force in self-defense. For example, Mencius advised the ruler of a small kingdom situated between two large kingdoms to build up his defenses to guard his people, and in case of an attack by one of his large neighbors, to be prepared to die in defense of his kingdom.[7]

Further, the above passages, while severely skeptical about the possibility of righteous wars undertaken by an individual state, leave open the possibility that some nondefensive wars might be just or at least morally better than others. These might include, as discussed in the next chapter, wars of humanitarian intervention.

# Christianity and
# the New Testament

In the New Testament, St. Paul's counsel to "if it is possible, so far as it depends on you, live peaceably with all" recommends the peaceful settlement of disputes. But it also seems to recognize cases in which it may be not be "possible," despite our best efforts, to preserve peace. Indeed, Jesus implied in certain verses that it is sometimes appropriate and necessary to use force. For example, he said to his apostles, "'The one who has a purse must take it, and likewise a bag. And the one who has no sword must sell his cloak and buy one. For I tell you, this scripture must be fulfilled in me.' . . . They said, 'Lord, look, here are two swords.' He replied, 'It is enough.'" And Jesus warned, "Do not think that I have come to bring peace to the earth; I have not come to bring peace, but a sword." In an encounter with a centurion Jesus notably did not ask him to give up his profession but instead praised his faith. And John the Baptist, when he met with soldiers, told them to "be satisfied with your wages"—a far cry from suggesting that to be a soldier is to engage in an ignoble occupation.[8]

According to one interpreter, the "attitude of the Gospels to the soldiers' calling was neutral. The centurion was commended for his faith rather than for his profession, but was not called upon to abandon his profession." Jesus himself defied the money changers in the temple in Jerusalem, pouring out their coins and overturning their tables.[9] These acts indicate a strong will to resist wrongdoing, including through physical force against property.

In light of these diverse passages, modern-day theologians have reached differing views about whether Jesus taught a strict principle of nonviolence. Some believe that he did. Others, like Reinhold Niebuhr, suggest that even if Jesus's teachings manifest an ethic of nonviolence and love, this ethic does not apply to relations among states in light of the reality of humanity's sinfulness. Many Christian ethicists have endorsed "just war" theories whose ethical forebears are the writings of St. Augustine and St. Thomas Aquinas. For example, St. Aquinas determined that three conditions must be satisfied for a war to be considered "just." First, "the ruler under whom the war is to be fought must have authority to do so." St. Aquinas asserted in this connection that sovereigns have a power to wage war to protect their people from foreign attacks. Second, "a just cause is required—so that those against whom the war is waged deserve such a response because of some offense on their part." Third, the sovereign must have "a right intention, to achieve some good or avoid some evil."[10]

Taking St. Aquinas's analysis as a point of departure, modern-day Christian just war theorists generally agree that a war, to qualify as "just," must meet the following criteria, as described by theologian Walter Wink: "1. The war must have a *just cause.* 2. It must be waged by a *legitimate authority.* 3. It must be *formally declared.* 4. It must be fought with a *peaceful intention.* 5. It must be *a last resort.* 6. There must be reasonable *hope of success.* 7. The means used must possess *proportionality* to the end sought." Wink also maintains that advocates of nonviolence and just war share certain beliefs in common, such as that "nonviolence is preferable to violence," that "the innocent must be protected as much as possible," that "any defense of a war motivated solely by a crusade mentality or national security interests or personal egocentricity" must be rejected, that states should be persuaded "to reduce the levels of violence," and that war must be held "accountable to moral values, both before and during the conflict."[11]

# Islam and the Koran

The Koran, while endorsing peace, establishes norms on the use of force, including on jihad. There is disagreement among scholars as to whether jihad is limited to defensive war because of ambiguous verses in the Koran. Many contemporary Muslim scholars believe that the principle of jihad articulated in the text of the Koran allows the use of force only in cases where it is necessary to defend oneself, one's community, or other individuals or communities. They cite verses explicitly prohibiting aggression, even against unbelievers who are opposed to the Muslim religion. For example, the Koran admonishes, "Let not detestation for a people who barred you from the Holy Mosque move you to commit aggression." It further asserts, "And fight in the way of God with those who fight with you, but aggress not: God loves not the aggressors." The Koran suggests that if the unbelievers cease their attacks, so also must Muslims: "If they withdraw from you, and do not fight you, and offer you peace, then God assigns not any way to you against them." However, if Muslims are attacked, then they should "slay" the unbelievers.[12]

Other interpreters (and modern-day terrorists acting in the name of Islam) have emphasized passages in the Koran that appear to endorse war against unbelievers even without an attack. For example, the Koran affirms, "When you meet the unbelievers, smite their necks, then, when you have made wide slaughter among them, tie fast the bonds; then set them free, either by grace or ransom, till the war lays down its loads." The Koran also states, "Fight those who believe not in God and the Last Day and do not forbid what God and His Messenger have forbidden—such men as practise not the religion of truth, being of those who have been given the Book—until they pay the tribute [poll tax] out of hand and have been humbled."[13]

Although the latter passages could be interpreted to authorize offensive war against unbelievers, some scholars believe that, when viewed in the context of the former passages prohibiting aggression, they presuppose a prior attack by the unbelievers. In the words of Rudolph Peters, in "those verses that seem to order the Muslims to fight the unbelievers unconditionally, the general condition that fighting is only allowed by way of defense could be said to be understood."[14]

# The Bahá'í Faith and the Bahá'í Writings

As noted in the preceding chapter, Bahá'u'lláh generally prohibited offensive war, including "holy war." He also advocated the establishment of a global collective security system. Further, 'Abdu'l-Bahá indicated that in some cases war, even by a single ruler, might be required as a last resort to stop an aggressor or end civil strife that was claiming the lives of innocent persons, and for the purpose of bringing about peace and respect for human rights. He thus endorsed a version of "just war":

A conquest can be a praiseworthy thing, and there are times when war becomes the powerful basis of peace, and ruin the very means of reconstruction. If, for example, a high-minded sovereign marshals his troops to block the onset of the insurgent and the aggressor, or again, if he takes the field and distinguishes himself in a struggle to unify a divided state and people, if, in brief, he is waging war for a righteous purpose, then this seeming wrath is mercy itself, and this apparent tyranny the very substance of justice and this warfare the cornerstone of peace. Today, the task befitting great rulers is to establish universal peace, for in this lies the freedom of all peoples.[15]

# Collective Security

Notably, passages from the scriptures of at least two of the religions considered in this book—Islam and the Bahá'í Faith—suggest that any decision to resort to the use of force against an aggressor or tyrant ideally ought to be made collectively. This decision should be made through consultation among all members of the community of individuals or nations that includes the aggressor and victim and all community members should support the enforcement action. This principle is often referred to as "collective security."

The Koran permits a community to resort to the collective use of force against a community member that attacks another. To recall the Koranic passage quoted earlier: "If two parties of the believers fight, put things right between them; then, if one of them is insolent against the other, fight the insolent one till it reverts to

God's commandment. If it reverts, set things right between them equitably, and be just." [16]

Bahá'u'lláh called upon the world's leaders to put in place a system of collective security after an inclusive and wide-ranging consultation among them:

> The time must come when the imperative necessity for the holding of a vast, an all embracing assemblage of men will be universally realized. The rulers and kings of the earth must needs attend it, and, participating in its deliberations, must consider such ways and means as will lay the foundations of the world's Great Peace amongst men. Such a peace demandeth that the Great Powers should resolve, for the sake of the tranquillity of the peoples of the earth, to be fully reconciled among themselves. Should any king take up arms against another, all should unitedly arise and prevent him. If this be done, the nations of the world will no longer require any armaments, except for the purpose of preserving the security of their realms and of maintaining internal order within their territories. This will ensure the peace and composure of every people, government and nation. [17]

# The Observance of Humanitarian Limitations on the Conduct of War

Passages from many of the scriptures provide rules for the humane conduct of military action. They suggest that any force used must be necessary and must be proportional to the moral goal sought to be achieved. Further, uses of force must not target civilians and particularly vulnerable individuals, including women and children. These passages thus clearly prohibit terrorist acts, which by their nature are designed to harm or kill innocent civilians.

As we have seen, the Bhagavad Gita endorses gentleness and compassion, which may apply in war as well as peace. The Hindu Code of Manu reflects these virtues and principles in a number of provisions. According to a prominent historian of international law, the Code of Manu displayed "an astounding degree of humaneness, if not softness, in matters of warfare. An honorable warrior is supposed, for instance, not to strike an enemy who is sleeping, or has lost his coat of arms, or is naked, or is overcome with grief, or has turned to flight."[18]

The Torah lays down various laws that regulate the way that any type of war is conducted. For example, even if a war is launched lawfully, the Book of Deuteronomy prohibits the destruction of fruit-bearing trees in the land that is taken over. Later interpreters, such as Maimonides, elaborated on this passage and clarified that it prohibits "wanton destruction." We have also seen that in optional wars the killing of women or children was not condoned. International legal historian Arthur Nussbaum has affirmed that Deuteronomy "contains what are probably the oldest written canons on warfare." Further, Maimonides established specific rules that permitted civilians to escape before an attack. Most rabbinical scholars believed that these rules applied only in optional wars, and not in obligatory wars."[19] From the requirement that civilians be allowed to seek refuge before an attack we can infer that noncombatants cannot be intentionally targeted.

Buddhist scriptures also stress that military actions must be conducted humanely. For example, a victor must treat a fallen adversary considerately: "If he moderates himself and, extinguishing all hatred in his heart lifts his down-trodden adversary up and says to him, 'Come now and make peace and let us be brothers,' he will gain a victory that is not a transient success, for its fruits will remain forever." We have seen that the Analects similarly condemns "cruelty" and endorses the abolition of "killing." It also requires soldiers to receive extensive moral training before being allowed to bear arms. These passages would appear to support humanitarian limits on how a just war may be pursued.[20]

The just war tradition that grew out of the teachings of the New Testament insisted on the observance of many humanitarian rules on the conduct of war. St. Augustine argued, for example, that prisoners should be treated with mercy. And St. Thomas Aquinas articulated a "principle of double effect." According to this principle, the morality of our acts is determined based on what we intend rather than on the unintended consequences of the acts. For example, if we kill an attacker in order to save our own life, producing the two effects of saving our life and killing the attacker, this action is judged legitimate because our intention is limited to saving our life, and killing the attacker is merely incidental to this legitimate intention. However, St. Aquinas maintained that even an "act that is prompted by a good intention can become illicit if it is not proportionate to the end intended." This qualification supported the evolution of humanitarian rules that require military action to be proportional to the intended objective. Moreover, contemporary theologians are in general agreement that under Christian just war theory, noncombatants must be granted immunity, prisoners must be treated fairly and humanely, and international agreements must be observed.[21]

The Koran, hadiths, and Islamic law establish many restrictions on how war is pursued aimed at protecting civilians. For example, the verse endorsing fighting against "those who fight with you" implies that the Koran only allows fighting against combatants. The

Koran also requires the feeding of the "captive." It mandates the release of prisoners, either by "grace or ransom," albeit after having achieved a victory by making "wide slaughter" among the unbelievers. Further, the Koran forbids aggression even against hated enemies and instead encourages us to help enemies "to piety and godfearing." According to various hadiths, Muḥammad prohibited killing women and children.[22]

A proclamation issued by the first caliph, Abu Bakr, "warns his victorious soldiers to spare women, children, and old men; he exhorts them not to destroy palms and orchards, or to burn homes, or to take from the provisions of the enemy more than needed, and he demands that prisoners of war be treated with pity." Historian Norman Bentwich maintained that "there is no doubt that the Arab rules of humanity in war influenced the Christian jurists of the fifteenth and sixteenth centuries in their attempts to introduce *temperamenta* into the warlike practices of the European States."[23]

The Bahá'í writings, too, encourage humane conduct in military action. 'Abdu'l-Bahá, for example, praised the services of individuals engaged in the Red Cross's humanitarian work during the First World War, and he repeatedly condemned inhumanity and cruelty in war. Bahá'u'lláh called for the conversion of weapons of war into "instruments of reconstruction."[24]

On the other hand, the Bahá'í writings imply that collective security actions undertaken on behalf of the world community must use adequate force against a government violating a collective security treaty to ensure it desists. In the words of 'Abdu'l-Bahá: "The fundamental principle underlying this solemn Pact should be so fixed that if any government later violate any one of its provisions, all the governments on earth should arise to reduce it to utter submission, nay the human race as a whole should resolve, with every power at its disposal, to destroy that government. Should this greatest of all remedies be applied to the sick body of the world, it will assuredly recover from its ills and will remain eternally safe and secure."[25] Notably, this passage contemplates the destruction only of the defaulting government, not innocent civilians.

# 15

# Intervention to Rescue Human Rights Victims

*If you refrained from rescuing those taken off to death, Those condemned to slaughter—If you say, 'We knew nothing of it,' Surely He who fathoms hearts will discern [the truth], He who watches over your life will know it, And He will pay each man as he deserves.*
                                                            —Proverbs 24:11–12

# Humanitarian Intervention in the Scriptures

In keeping with the general ethical obligation to rescue the oppressed as well as principles regarding the legitimate use of force, passages from many of the scriptures permit the measured use of force to rescue victims of human rights violations. The use of force to rescue such victims is often referred to as "humanitarian intervention." The scriptures suggest that there are moral duties of humanitarian intervention that apply to everyone, from an individual to an entire nation.

# Hinduism and the Bhagavad Gita

The Bhagavad Gita does not specifically address the subject of intervention to rescue human rights victims. However, the virtues that it endorses would support a principle of humanitarian intervention. These include virtues of "generosity" and "compassion towards creatures." One way of showing compassion to those in distress is to rescue them. Further, although the Gita promotes a broad ethic of "harmlessness," its battle setting implicitly acknowledges a role for the just use of military force, as we noted in the preceding chapter. Humanitarian intervention might constitute such a legitimate use of force.[1]

# Judaism and the Hebrew Scriptures

The Hebrew scriptures and Jewish law approve of the calculated use of force to rescue those who are in peril or are persecuted. According to the Torah, Jews must not "profit by the blood of your fellow." Rabbis have understood this passage to require Jews not to "stand idly by" when their neighbors are threatened. Moses himself struck down and killed an Egyptian who was beating a Hebrew. We have seen that a verse in Psalms states, "Judge the wretched and the orphan, vindicate the lowly and the poor, rescue the wretched and the needy; save them from the hand of the wicked." According to another verse, kings are obligated to rescue "the needy who cry out" and "the lowly who have no helper." Job affirms that this obligation to save others applies to foreigners as well as countrymen who are in need of help: "I was a father to the needy, And I looked into the case of the stranger." Moreover, a verse in Proverbs implies that we cannot plead ignorance as a justification for shirking our obligation to save a person in imminent danger of being killed: "If you refrained from rescuing those taken off to death, Those condemned to slaughter—If you say, 'We knew nothing of it,' Surely He who fathoms hearts will discern [the truth], He who watches over your life will know it, And He will pay each man as he deserves."[2]

The Code of Maimonides lays down detailed rules for implementing our obligation to rescue others:

If one person is able to save another and does not save him, he transgresses the commandment, *Neither shalt thou stand idly by the blood of thy neighbor.* . . . Similarly, if one person sees another drowning in the sea, or being attacked by bandits, or being attacked by wild animals, and although able to rescue him either alone or by hiring others, does not rescue him; . . . or if one acts in any similar way—he transgresses in each case the injunction, *Neither shalt thou stand idly by the blood of thy neighbor.*[3]

Rabbis ruled that a Jew is required to violate any commandment except for those against idolatry, sexual offenses, or murder to save a human life. Maimonides recognized that it may be necessary to kill a person pursuing another in order to save the life of the individual being stalked: "If one person is pursuing another with the intention of killing him, even if the pursuer is a minor, it is the duty of every Israelite to save the pursued, even at the cost of the pursuer's life." But he insisted that if it was possible to rescue a victim only by injuring the pursuer so as to incapacitate him, then "this should be done." At the same time, Maimonides ruled that an attacker could be killed if necessary in order to protect a victim in imminent danger: "If, however, it is impossible to judge exactly and the pursued can be rescued only if the pursuer is killed, he may be killed even though he has not yet killed anyone."[4]

Under Jewish law the obligation to rescue others applies to kings and nations in addition to individuals. According to legal scholar Michael J. Broyde, rabbinical commentators accordingly recognized a third category of war (alongside obligatory and optional wars) grounded in the obligation to protect victims against a pursuer. Under this kind of rationale, a nation could rightfully undertake humanitarian intervention and also engage in self-defense. Broyde emphasizes, however, that under Jewish law very strict rules must be observed. In particular, a defender may not (1) "kill an innocent third party to save a life"; (2) "compel a person to risk his life to save the life of another"; (3) "kill the pursuer after his evil act is over as a form of punishment"; and (4) "use more force than is minimally needed." Broyde believes, therefore, that "the rules of this type of 'armed conflict' would resemble the activities of a police force rather than the activities of an army."[5]

# Buddhism and Buddhist Scriptures

We saw in the preceding chapter that Buddhist scriptures, while promoting peace, allow for the possibility of just wars waged for "a righteous cause after having exhausted all means to preserve the peace."[6] In light of the Buddha's teachings of compassion, love for others, and selflessness, these just wars could include military action to rescue human rights victims.

# Confucianism and the Works of Mencius

The writings of Mencius support an inference, in the words of one scholar, that the "Confucians would approve the use of force by one state against another state for the protection against abusive rule in the latter if properly carried out." For example, Mencius's writings describe an incident in which the people of Qi attacked the state of Yan and conquered it. The ruler of Yan was "tyrannizing over his people" and the people of Yan welcomed the invasion. The ruler of Qi asked for Mencius's advice about whether he should take possession of Yan after the invasion. Mencius advised him to take possession of Yan if this would please the people of Yan. He also recommended, however, that the ruler not take possession of Yan if the population of Yan was not in favor of having a new ruler. Mencius explained to the ruler of Qi that the people of Yan welcomed the invasion with "baskets of rice and vessels of congee" because they hoped to escape the oppression they had suffered. But he warned the ruler of Qi that if he made the people's oppression worse, they would rebel against his leadership.

Shortly afterwards the ruler of Qi took possession of the state of Yan. But instead of working to improve the condition of the people of Yan, he killed their fathers and elder brothers and imprisoned their sons and younger brothers. He also destroyed a temple and looted precious vessels from it.

Mencius sharply criticized these actions and the failure of the ruler of Qi to "put in practice a benevolent government." He said that it was understandable that Yan and its allies would try to repel Qi after its invasion. He advised the ruler of Qi that the only way to stop the threatened attack by Yan and its allies was to free his prisoners—both old and young—to stop the looting of the precious vessels, and, after consulting with the people of Yan, to appoint a ruler for them and "withdraw from the country."

Through this account Mencius stressed that humanitarian intervention may be permissible if it is welcomed by human rights victims and results in relief from their oppression and an improvement in their welfare. His writings furthermore imply that he viewed warfare as "*only* justified when it is in the nature of 'humanitarian intervention.'"[7]

# Christianity and the New Testament

There are many different opinions among Christian theologians about the legitimacy of humanitarian intervention. In particular, theologians have disagreed about how to harmonize Jesus's general advocacy of nonviolence with his teachings to practice Good Samaritanism, especially in situations where the use of force appears to be required to defend and protect innocent victims. Some have argued that nonviolent methods should be pursued even in the case of an attack on an innocent person. They have emphasized in this connection that Jesus himself intervened to prevent the stoning of an adulteress by verbal admonitions to the woman's oppressors rather than by the use of force.[8]

Other theologians have taken the position that the moral imperative of defending an innocent victim may require the threat or use of force. For example, theologian Paul Ramsey wrote, "What do you imagine Jesus would have had the Samaritan do if in the story he had come upon the scene when the robbers had just begun their attack and while they were still at their fell work? Would it not then be a work of charity to resort to the only available and effective means of preventing or punishing the attack and resisting the injustice? Is not anyone *obliged* to do this if he can?" Accordingly, many modern-day Christian ethicists have endorsed the legitimacy of humanitarian intervention.[9]

# Islam and the Koran

There are several passages from the Koran that appear to approve of humanitarian intervention and even require it as a moral duty.

For example, the Koran demands, "How is it with you, that you do not fight in the way of God, and for the men, women, and children, who, being abased, say, 'Our Lord, bring us forth from this city whose people are evildoers, and appoint to us a protector from Thee, and appoint to us from Thee a helper'?" One scholar believes that because the Koran exalts each and every human being, it "places the unconditional duty to save human life above all else; for to save one is to save all, the infinitude of men in this man, the blood of all the ages in his blood." And a hadith permits preventing aggression. The hadith states, "Help your brother whether he is an aggressor or a victim of aggression." When asked how an aggressor should be helped, Muḥammad answers, "By preventing him from carrying out his aggression as best you can." Based on these authorities and principles, many contemporary scholars have argued that there is an Islamic ethic of humanitarian intervention.[10]

# The Bahá'í Faith and the Bahá'í Writings

'Abdu'l-Bahá interpreted Jesus's counsel to "turn the other [cheek] also"[11] as intended to teach us not to seek personal revenge and to forgive those who wrong us. However, he maintained, Jesus did not mean to prohibit us from preventing harm to *others* by restraining a wrongdoer:

Then what Christ meant by forgiveness and pardon is not that, when nations attack you, burn your homes, plunder your goods, assault your wives, children and relatives, and violate your honor, you should be submissive in the presence of these tyrannical foes and allow them to perform all their cruelties and oppressions. No, the words of Christ refer to the conduct of two individuals toward each other: if one person assaults another, the injured one should forgive him. But the communities must protect the rights of man. So if someone assaults, injures, oppresses and wounds me, I will offer no resistance, and I will forgive him. But if a person wishes to assault [someone else], certainly I will prevent him.[12]

In keeping with this teaching, the Bahá'í writings strongly emphasize duties to protect the rights of others and defend them against tyranny and oppression. For example, Bahá'u'lláh exhorted all of us to be "'an upholder and defender of the victim of oppression.'"[13] A passage from Bahá'u'lláh's writings, quoted in chapter 14, might be read to support collective military action for the purpose of protecting individuals from despotism. The passage reads:

Should any king take up arms against another, all should unitedly arise and prevent him. If this be done, the nations of the world will no longer require any armaments, except for the purpose of preserving the security of their realms and of maintaining internal order within their territories. This will ensure the peace and composure of every people, government and nation. We fain would hope that the kings and rulers of the earth, the mirrors of the gracious and almighty name of God, may attain unto this station, and shield mankind from the onslaught of tyranny.[14]

The Bahá'í writings envision a future age in which this principle of collective security, including its protections against tyranny, will be applied worldwide by agreement of the world's leaders.

# 16

## Optimism and Pragmatism

*Be perfect, therefore, as your heavenly Father is perfect.*

—Jesus

Philosophers and political scientists have identified three broad views of human behavior, which in turn affect our determination of what is the ethical course of action. The first is an optimistic view, which holds that we should be optimistic about the human capacity for moral behavior. This kind of perspective might lead us to be very demanding in establishing high ethical standards for conduct. A second view is pessimistic about the human capacity for moral behavior. This view might lead us to tolerate, or even advocate, "unethical" conduct, because it would be unreasonable to expect more virtuous conduct from fallible humans. The third view is pragmatic about our ability to behave uprightly. A pragmatic or realistic view might lead us to formulate broad ethical standards but recognize that their implementation may be progressive because of the need to take human weaknesses into account.[1]

This categorization of perspectives helps to illuminate the ethical approach of the scriptures. There is a fundamental optimism in the scriptures regarding our ability as humans, through turning to divine revelation or moral principles, to transform our own behavior and that of social institutions. These optimistic views stand in stark contrast to some pessimistic political and social theories, which presume that we are hopelessly selfish. However, many passages from the scriptures also have a pragmatic emphasis. They acknowledge the critical social functions of governments and accept the realities of political power, but they also seek to change many of these realities. And there is a pessimistic element in most of the scriptures in their assessment of the current moral state of the world and in their view of the consequences for human civilization should we fail to adopt a moral outlook. But this sober view is never allowed to undercut our moral duty to endeavor to fulfill fundamental moral values in our lives. For these reasons the scriptures are essentially optimistic and pragmatic.

Turning to examples from specific scriptures, the Bhagavad Gita's emphasis on spiritual transformation reflects a certain optimism. At the same time, the Gita pragmatically recognizes the justness, at times, of fighting. Similarly, the Torah's teaching that God created humans in His own image evidences a belief that we can indeed develop spiritual virtues: "You shall be holy, for I, the Lord your God, am holy." But the Hebrew scriptures are also practical in their injunctions to obey governments out of recognition of their *de facto* authority: "One who obeys orders will not suffer from the dangerous situation."[2]

The outlook of Buddhist scriptures is likewise fundamentally optimistic. They maintain that individuals and society can evolve for the better over time through constant striving to live according to moral principles. But while idealistic, Buddhist scriptures are also realistic. For example, they counsel us to "do good deeds, and try to win mindfulness!" at the same time that they recognize that "those who go to war in a righteous cause after having exhausted all means to preserve the peace are [not] blameworthy." In the words of one scholar, the "Buddhist ideology is pragmatic in so far as it is to serve as a basis for action, its view of life pointing to a way of life. ... The task of Buddhism is therefore to help man transform himself from what he is to what he ought to be." And the same scholar asserts that the Buddha advocated "a dynamic evolutionary conception of society."[3]

In the Analects, Confucius was hopeful in the long run about our ability to cultivate humaneness through appropriate motivation and volition. He said, "Is *rŭn* really far away? If I want *rŭn,* then *rén* is already there." He taught that ultimately we must nurture within ourselves a desire to achieve humaneness, rather than expect only others to reform their characters. Confucius stated, "If he makes his own duties heavy, and asks less of others, he will keep resentment at a distance. . . . One who does not say, 'What is to be done, what is to be done'—I don't know *what* is to be done with him!" But Confucius was also realistic in his counsels to individuals to fulfill their prescribed social roles, affirming, "The ruler is a ruler, the minister is a minister, the father is a father, the son is a son." [4]

Jesus's teachings in the New Testament also manifest an optimism about the human capacity for transcendent love despite the pervasiveness of sin. Jesus's injunction to "be perfect, therefore, as your heavenly Father is perfect" reflects this optimism. So does St. Paul's counsel to "not be conformed to this world, but be transformed by the renewing of your minds." At the same time, as we have seen, St. Paul announced a general principle of obedience to secular rulers, which showed a practical way of thinking. In this connection, the Christian theologian Reinhold Niebuhr argued that Christianity calls for a "qualified optimism." [5]

According to Muslim scholar Fazlur Rahman, the Koran is ultimately sanguine about our ability to act morally: "On the whole, despite the sad accounts of the human record in the Qur'ān, its attitude is quite optimistic with regard to the sequel of human endeavor." But again, the Koran contains various pragmatic injunctions, including the injunction to obey authorities: "O believers, . . . obey the Messenger and those in authority among you." [6]

The Bahá'í writings, too, are confident about the long-term prospects for creating a world that is both politically and spiritually united. At the same time, they require us to take practical action toward unity. In the words of 'Abdu'l-Bahá, "Results follow action. Mere theory is fruitless. Of what use is a book upon medicine if it is never taken from the library shelf? When practical activity has been manifested, the teachings of God have borne fruit." Further, the Bahá'í writings are clear-eyed about the short-term tribulations that may have to precede world unification. For example, Bahá'u'lláh wrote soberly, "The winds of despair are, alas, blowing from every direction, and the strife that divideth and afflicteth the human race is daily increasing. The signs of impending convulsions and chaos can now be discerned, inasmuch as the prevailing order appeareth to be lamentably defective." Nevertheless, he promised that war and strife ultimately will be overcome through our persistent efforts. He assured us, "'These fruitless strifes, these ruinous wars shall pass away and the "Most Great Peace" shall come.'"[7]

# 17

## The Prospects for a Global Ethic

*Religion is verily the chief instrument for the establishment of order in the world and of tranquillity amongst its peoples.*

—Bahá'u'lláh

# The Prospects for a Global Ethic Based on Shared Ethical Principles

This book has demonstrated that selected passages from the foundational scriptures of seven world religions can be interpreted to support certain shared ethical principles. The recognition of these common principles in each religion's scriptures does not in any way detract from the unique qualities of each religion, including the life of its founder and the body of writings, traditions, and laws that are revered by its believers. Instead, the gradual recognition of the common ethical themes that run through all the scriptures can help bridge differences and divisions between members of different faiths as well as resolve the ethical dilemmas highlighted in chapter 1.

Numerous conferences bringing together representatives of these and other faiths have recognized the existence of these shared principles. For example, the participants in the first World Conference on Religion and Peace, held in Kyoto, Japan, in 1970, agreed on a list of common moral teachings. These teachings include, among others, "A conviction of the fundamental unity of the human family, and the equality and dignity of all human beings; A sense of the sacredness of the individual person and his conscience; A sense of the value of human community; . . . A

sense of obligation to stand on the side of the poor and the oppressed as against the rich and the oppressors; and A profound
hope that good will finally prevail." And in 1993 the Parliament
of the World's Religions adopted a *Declaration Toward a Global
Ethic,* which articulates similar common beliefs among the world
religions.[1]

Modern-day scholars of comparative religion have also recognized this congruence of ethical principles among the world religions. For example, Huston Smith has referred to the ethics of the
Ten Commandments, the virtues of humility, charity, and verac-
ity, and a vision of a more integrated world as being common beliefs of the world's major religions. And political scientist Samuel P.
Huntington, in the conclusion of his book *The Clash of Civilizations,* suggests that "whatever the degree to which they divided humankind, the world's major religions—Western Christianity, Or-
thodoxy, Hinduism, Buddhism, Islam, Confucianism, Taoism, Judaism—also share key values in common. If humans are ever to
develop a universal civilization, it will emerge gradually through
the exploration and expansion of these commonalities."[2]

More importantly, there is evidence that these shared ethical
principles are in fact supported by many devout believers of diverse faiths, although obviously not by those who preach religious
antagonism. A fair-minded examination of the scriptures demonstrates that those who adopt the rhetoric of religious tradition in
the service of hatred are not following the fundamental ethical
precepts that are found in the scriptures of their own religion.
The fact that so many believers of the world's religions today sub-
scribe to these fundamental principles and are trying to implement them in their personal lives certainly increases the chances
that a global ethic may soon be achievable.

# Implications of Shared Ethical Principles for Contemporary Ethical Dilemmas

The shared principles in the world's religious scriptures have a number of implications for the ethical problems, highlighted in Chapter 1, that are facing our despairing world. In particular, they suggest the primacy of an ethical principle of "unity in diversity." According to this principle, our primary allegiance morally ought to be to the entire human family rather than to our own country or to a particular ethnic, racial, or religious group, even though we should also value these lesser affiliations.

The Golden Rule is a universal principle that we too often ignore in practice but that can open the door to new ways of thinking about a wide variety of contemporary ethical problems. At a minimum, it implies that we have higher moral obligations to others than simply refraining from interfering with their freedom. And the Golden Rule requires deeds, not just pious words. For example, in responding to various humanitarian crises around the globe, governments have too often uttered high-minded rhetoric rather than taking concrete action to help the victims.

The sacred scriptures also instruct us to cultivate particular virtues, including kindness, generosity, and selflessness. According to these writings, we have compelling obligations to help, to the best of our abilities, those less fortunate than ourselves. Needless to say, many aspects of Western culture, and in particular its emphasis on material acquisitiveness, fail to reflect these virtues. And long-term solutions to destructive conflicts must ultimately depend on the ability of affected individuals to develop and demonstrate the virtues of forgiveness and just-mindedness toward members of other groups.

The world's religious scriptures emphasize the fundamental equality of all human beings rather than any inherent superiority of particular groups, despite the sordid history of religious fanaticism and hatred. They support the modern concept of universal human rights and demand that everyone enjoy these rights, whatever our race, ethnicity, nationality, or religion. They place particular emphasis on the moral responsibilities of all of us as individuals—not just governments—to implement these rights by treating all other human beings with compassion and respect.

The sacred scriptures of the world's religions suggest the primacy of not only rights to life and physical security but also a right to subsistence. Furthermore, they endorse freedom of religion and conscience, as well as the fundamental spiritual equality of women and men. More recent scriptures point to the need to enhance the social status of women. And the scriptures insist that the primary function of all governments is to uphold the human rights of people and to govern in their interests.

The scriptures reviewed in this book support the resolution of problems through a fair and impartial process of open-minded consultation—a process that is all too rare in resolving conflicts, especially those within and between governments. Instead, parties either resort to force or the threat of force, or they rely exclusively on more traditional mechanisms like bargaining or majority voting. By contrast, consultation, even though it may be followed by voting, involves a far more proactive process in which we enthusiastically seek out and thoughtfully consider diverse opinions in an effort to achieve a best answer that will unify rather than divide. The ethical concept of consultation deserves to be studied far more rigorously to discover ways in which we and world leaders can apply it more expansively in various arenas of individual, national, and international relations.

The ideal of open-minded consultation is related to the shared principle of respect for governments and law. Today countless aggrieved groups are making claims to overturn the established government or legal system, often by force. The passages from the world's scriptures reviewed here suggest that these claims must always be viewed as counterproductive, for by their very nature they promote disunity and risk further conflict. But the scriptures also imply that rebellion may be necessary, in very extreme cases, as an absolute last resort. Accordingly, shared principles in religious scriptures would support the development of imaginative and peaceful solutions to the many demands for autonomy being lodged by diverse national, ethnic, and religious groups in the contemporary world. These solutions could include the creation of innovative federal structures that might allow aggrieved groups a significant degree of decision-making freedom, while also promoting respect for a central government.

The scriptures also endorse the peaceful resolution of all kinds of disputes. At the same time, they recognize the intimate interdependence of peace and justice, including respect for universal human rights. In short, they demand that the governments of the world continue to strive to bring about a just peace in troubled parts of the globe and not settle for a minimal peace that represents simply a cessation of active hostilities. They also demand that governments respect their treaty obligations and recognize this respect as a moral duty. And the sacred texts of most religions point to the need for governments to continue to develop international law and cooperation among nations.

While the scriptures reviewed in this book thus strongly emphasize the importance of building a just and durable peace throughout the world, founded on respect for international law and treaty commitments, they also recognize that the use of force is sometimes necessary to preserve peace between individuals and nations. But they suggest that the only legitimate purposes for the use of force between states are to protect states or individuals or to achieve other limited goals demanded by justice. The Bahá'í writings and the Koran in particular point to the desirability of establishing a system of collective security that would protect individuals as well as states. At the same time, the scriptures require that any party engaging in legitimate uses of force must scrupulously avoid targeting civilians, and they suggest that every possible effort must be made to protect them from injury or death. Many scriptural passages mandate that prisoners be treated humanely. They unequivocally condemn terrorist acts, which by definition are deliberately and ruthlessly aimed at killing or maiming innocent people. They thus imply that governments must strengthen the international law of armed conflict and international law concerning the prevention, suppression, and punishment of terrorism.

The scriptures also recognize that one legitimate purpose of using force is the protection of human beings who are the victims of tyranny or other forms of severe human rights violations. In fact, they underscore that individuals have an unquestionable and clear-cut duty to rescue others in distress and imply that states likewise have compelling duties to come to the aid of human rights victims, ideally by working with one another pursuant to open-minded consultation. The scriptures thus unequivocally support the concept of humanitarian intervention and suggest that the global community must develop new ways to ensure that appropriate intervention occurs early in a human rights crisis before greater tragedies unfold.

More generally, the scriptures of the world's major religions suggest that we should be optimistic about the human capacity for ethical behavior and that we therefore have a duty to undertake the reforms described above. They imply, at the same time, that we need to be pragmatic about our approach to implementing these reforms and that we need to be realistic in our expectations. At a minimum, the sacred texts of the religions reject any form of cynicism or complacency about the current condition of human affairs.

# The Potential Influence of Religion and Religious Scriptures

A global ethic based on shared principles in religious scriptures has a special potential to motivate humanitarian endeavors by individuals from all walks of life. In the words of one scholar, the "great potential in world religions is that they can reach peoples around the globe more directly and more fully than any other societal institution." Indeed, the shared ethical principles explored in this book have inspired many individuals and organizations with a religious identification to work diligently to promote peace, including peace between and among contending religious communities. These individuals and organizations have the unique opportunity, according to another scholar, to "appeal to the parties on the basis of universal religious principles or on the basis of the specific warrants for conflict resolution that exist in each religion's theology."[3] Moreover, nongovernmental organizations with a religious affiliation have often been among the most reliable supporters of global humanitarian aid and assistance. They have been inspired by fundamental moral teachings of the unity of humankind and the duty to provide succor to the less fortunate.

Further, studies undertaken by sociologists and psychologists have identified a positive relationship between "the internalization of [the] central teachings" of religion and freedom from racial, ethnic, or national prejudice. For example, psychologist Gordon Allport concluded, in his highly regarded 1950 study, *The Nature of Prejudice*, that religious believers who adopted the ethnocentric attitudes of institutionalized religion were more prejudiced than believers who had internalized the principles of the Golden Rule and the "brotherhood of man." Allport stated that these principles were shared by all the great world religions and promoted tolerance among those religious followers who attempted to live according to them.[4]

Agreement on shared principles in the world's religious scriptures will only be achievable, however, through a willingness among members of different religious communities to reinvestigate their scriptures and faiths with an open-minded attitude in order to find these points of commonality. This process itself must be grounded in a spiritual sense of unity and good will. Rigid adherence to traditional dogmas without unprejudiced inquiry will only perpetuate the gross divisions that have too often marred relations among religious communities and their ability to work together to promote shared moral values. Moreover, the cultivation of a global ethic will require a new readiness among individuals of different faiths, and of no faith, to consult with one another to come to better understandings of the core beliefs they have in common.

I hope that this book will help to inspire readers to explore the common ethical principles that the scriptures of the world religions promote. My goal is to motivate both believers and nonbelievers to engage in a new search, based on these principles, for solutions to the many vexing social problems that now engender so much despair throughout the globe. Most importantly, I hope that we will come to feel a moral obligation to embark on this journey because of our recognition that we are all, as the world's great scriptures have so eloquently affirmed, members of one human family. In the words of 'Abdu'l-Bahá: "All peoples and nations are of one family, the children of one Father, and should be to one another as brothers and sisters!"[5]

# Notes

# 1 / Is There Hope
# for a Global Ethic?

1. For a review of contemporary conflicts and global trends in violent conflict, see Marshall and Gurr, *Peace and Conflict 2005*.

2. See UN Millennium Project, *Investing in Development*, pp. 1–23.

3. For an example of a work generally defending cultural relativism, see Pollis, "Cultural Relativism Revisited"; Huntington, *Clash of Civilizations*.

4. For a collection of essays reflecting differing opinions on the legality of the Iraq war under the UN Charter, see Damrosch and Oxman et al., "Agora: Future Implications of the Iraq Conflict."

5. Franck, *Power of Legitimacy*, pp. 235–36.

6. On the spread of religious nationalism after the Cold War, see Juergensmeyer, *New Cold War?*

7. Smart and Hecht, *Sacred Texts of the World*, pp. xi, xiii.

8. See "Worldwide Adherents of All Religions by Six Continental Areas, Mid-2003." According to figures in the *2004 Encyclopedia Britannica Book of the Year*, the eight largest religions in descending rank order are as follows, including the percentage that their followers represented of the total world population in mid-2003 (6.288 billion): Christianity—2.070 billion, or 32.9 percent; Islam—1.254 billion, or 19.9 percent; Hinduism—837 million, or 13.3 percent; Confucianism and Chinese Universism—405 million, or 6.4 percent; Buddhism—373 million, or 5.9 percent; Sikhism—24 million, or 0.4 percent; Judaism—15 million, or 0.2 percent; the Bahá'í Faith—8 million, or 0.1 percent. (All figures are rounded to the nearest million.) Despite Sikhism's ranking as the sixth largest religion, I have not included it because of the relatively small geographic distribution of its members, who reside in only thirty-four countries according to the *2004 Encyclopedia Britannica Book of the Year*. All of the above figures are approximate. For example, the Bahá'í World Center gives a more conservative estimate of 5 million for the current number of Bahá'ís worldwide. See www.bahai.org for more information.

9. For background information on Hinduism, see Zaehner, *Hinduism*; see especially ibid., pp. 3, 93; Sharma, "Hinduism," p. 33.

10. Bhagavad Gita 4.8; see also Bhagavad Gita 10.14, 11.47, 4.7. All quotations from or references to the Bhagavad Gita are from the translation by Franklin Edgerton. See Edgerton, trans., *Bhagavad Gītā*.

11. The quoted words of Moses are from Exodus 18:16; unless otherwise noted, all quotations from or references to the Hebrew scriptures are from *Tanakh*; on subsequent rabbinical writings see Goodman, "The Individual and the Community," pp. 36–46.

12. For background information on Buddhist scriptures, see Conze, *Buddhist Scriptures*, pp. 11–16. This compilation contains many of these widely-revered scriptures.

13. The quotation on the title of the Buddha is found in Nagarjuna, "Mahaprajnaparamitashastra," in Conze, *Buddhist Scriptures*, p. 30; on the life of the Bud-

dha, see Ashvaghosha, "Buddhacarita," in Conze, *Buddhist Scriptures*, pp. 34–66; the quotation from the Buddha on nirvana is found in Ashvaghosha, "Buddhacarita," in Conze, *Buddhist Scriptures*, pp. 53–54.

14. See Irene Bloom, correspondence with the author dated July 13–14, 1998; see Brooks and Brooks, *Original Analects*, for all subsequent quotations from or references to the Analects; the quotation regarding the revered character of the Analects is found in Wei-ming, "Confucianism," p. 183.

15. All quotations from or references to the New Testament are from *The Holy Bible Containing the Old and New Testaments: New Revised Standard Version*; John 10:30, 14:9; the quotations and information on the books of the New Testament are found in Smart and Hecht, *Sacred Texts of the World*, p. 91; the quotation on Christian groups acknowledging the authority of the New Testament is found in Langan, "The Individual and the Collectivity," p. 155.

16. Koran 41:5; all quotations from or references to the Koran are from the translation of A. J. Arberry, and verses are numbered according to the system used in his translation (see Arberry, *The Koran Interpreted*); on Islamic jurisprudence and law, see Schacht, *An Introduction to Islamic Law*.

17. For a more detailed history of the Bahá'í Faith and summary of its teachings, see Hatcher and Martin, *The Bahá'í Faith: The Emerging Global Religion*.

18. In addition to Noah, Abraham, Moses, Jesus, and Muḥammad, the Bahá'í writings also recognize Krishna, the Buddha, and Zoroaster as Manifestations of God. They further regard Confucius as a great moral teacher. See, for example, 'Abdu'l-Bahá, *Promulgation of Universal Peace*, p. 346; 'Abdu'l-Bahá, *Some Answered Questions*, pp. 47, 165; 'Abdu'l-Bahá, *Paris Talks*, nos. 9.1–3. For the Bahá'í view of the validity of other religions, see Bahá'u'lláh, *Gleanings*, p. 217.

19. 'Abdu'l-Bahá, *Some Answered Questions*, pp. 47, 48.

# 2 / Unity in Diversity

The epigraph for chapter 2 is from Bhagavad Gita 5.18.

1. Bhagavad Gita 5.7, 11.7; Sastry, "Hinduism and International Law," p. 552.

2. Leviticus 19:18; Malachi 2:10; on the covenant between God and Moses and the Israelites, see Exodus 19; on the Noachide covenant, see Genesis 8:20–9:19; on both covenants, see Cartwright, "Biblical Argument in International Ethics," pp. 272–73.

3. Ashvaghosha, "Buddhacarita," in Conze, *Buddhist Scriptures*, p. 55; Conze, *Buddhist Scriptures*, p. 186; on the teaching that mankind belongs to one species, see Salgado, "Equality and Inequality," p. 60.

4. Analects 12.5.

5. For the story of the Good Samaritan, see Luke 10:25–37.

6. Romans 10:12; Galatians 3:28; Philippians 3:20; Ephesians 2:14–15, 2:19.

7. Koran 4:1, 17:72, 2:208, 10:20, 21:93; the hadith quoted in the text is from

Weeramantry, *Islamic Jurisprudence*, p. 133; on the principle of the oneness of human-kind in Islam, see ibid., p. 133.

8. Bahá'u'lláh, *Tablets of Bahá'u'lláh*, p. 167; Bahá'u'lláh, *Gleanings*, p. 286; Shoghi Effendi, *World Order of Bahá'u'lláh*, p. 202.

9. Bhagavad Gita 5.18; on the comparison to the biblical injunction, see Edgerton, "Interpretation of the Bhagavad Gītā," pp. 162–63.

10. Ezekiel 5:5–6; Isaiah 19:24–25.

11. Bentwich, *Religious Foundations of Internationalism*, pp. 62–63.

12. On the prescription of various duties in Buddhism, see de Silva, "The Concept of Equality," pp. 81–82; the quotation from the Buddha regarding relatives is from Ashvaghosha, "Saundaranandakavya," in Conze, *Buddhist Scriptures*, pp. 110–11; for further reading on the Buddha's teachings on the love of one's country, see de Silva, "The Concept of Equality," p. 89; the quotation from the Buddha regarding the safety of countries is taken from Ashvaghosha, "Saundaranandakavya," in Conze, *Buddhist Scriptures*, p. 111; the quotation on racial feelings is from Jayatilleke, "The Principles of International Law in Buddhist Doctrine," p. 498.

13. On Confucius's teachings on respect for parents and siblings, see Analects 1.2, 1.6–7, 2.20–21, 4.18; the quotation on filiality is from Analects 1.2; the quotation beginning "The ruler is a ruler" is from Analects 12.11.

14. Analects 13.19; the quotation on a "claim of universality" is from Brooks and Brooks, *Original Analects*, p. 102; the quotation from Mencius is found in Legge, *Works of Mencius*, 1:1:7, p. 143; the quotation by a twentieth-century scholar is from Bentwich, *Religious Foundations of Internationalism*, p. 196.

15. For examples of passages from the letters of St. Paul and St. Peter regarding duties in particular social relationships, see Colossians 3:18–25 and 1 Peter 2:13–3:17; St. Paul's quotation on loving family members is found in 1 Timothy 5:8; Jesus's injunction on loyalty to the emperor is found in Matthew 22:21; on St. Paul's letter to the Romans, see Romans 13:1–7; the quotation regarding Jesus's teachings on human dignity is found in Preston, "Christian Ethics," p. 104.

16. Koran 49:13, 30:21, 5:53; on the Koran's endorsement of the "positive value of different religions and communities," see Rahman, *Major Themes of the Qur'ān*, p. 167.

17. Shoghi Effendi, *World Order of Bahá'u'lláh*, pp. 41–42.

# 3 / The Golden Rule and the Importance of Good Deeds

The epigraph for chapter 3 is from Matthew 7:12.

1. For more comprehensive and sophisticated analyses of the formulation and application of the Golden Rule in various religious and philosophical systems, see Rost, *Golden Rule*, and Wattles, *Golden Rule*. On some of the difficulties of using the Golden

Rule as a moral standard in the absence of the types of caveats described in the text, see Gewirth, "The Golden Rule Rationalized."

2. The quotations comparing the ethical doctrines of the Gita to the Golden Rule are from Edgerton, "Interpretation of the Bhagavad Gītā," pp. 185, 191; Bhagavad Gita: 6.32, 13.28.

3. Leviticus 19:18; Rabbi Hillel's formulation of the Golden Rule is from B. T. Shabbat 31a, quoted in Kellner, "Jewish Ethics," pp. 86–87; on the Torah's teaching that God created humans in His own image, see Genesis 1:27, 5:1; the quotation on holiness is from Leviticus 19:2.

4. "Udana," in Conze, *Buddhism,* p. 61; ibid., pp. 61–62.

5. Analects 15.24, 12.22, 6.30 (emphasis in original); the reference to cultivated judgment is from Hall and Ames, *Thinking Through Confucius,* pp. 116–17.

6. Matthew 22:37–40, 7:12; Philippians 2:3–4; Galatians 6:10.

7. Koran 59:9; Bahá'u'lláh, Kitáb-i-Íqán, ¶214; Bahá'u'lláh, *Tablets of Bahá'u'lláh,* pp. 64, 71.

8. On meditation, see Bhagavad Gita 6.10–15; Bhagavad Gita 3.14, 7.28, 6.46; on hypocrisy, see Bhagavad Gita 16.4, 16.10; on the Bhagavad Gita's opposition to asceticism, see Edgerton, "Interpretation of the Bhagavad Gītā," pp. 131, 158–61.

9. Deuteronomy 16:20; Psalms 82:4.

10. Ashvaghosha, "Buddhacarita," in Conze, *Buddhist Scriptures,* p. 62; on a middle path, see ibid., pp. 55–56; Analects 14.27, 2.24.

11. Matthew 23:1–3.

12. Koran 4:97; Bahá'u'lláh, *Gleanings,* p. 305; 'Abdu'l-Bahá, *Paris Talks,* no. 1.10.

# 4 / Personal Virtues
# and Moral Duties

The epigraph for chapter 4 is from Bhagavad Gita 16.1–3.

1. Bhagavad Gita 12.13, 16.2; Exodus 23:9; Carus, *Gospel of Buddha,* p. 148.

2. See Analects 1.6, 17.5; Analects 14.34; on the interpretation of Analects 14.34, see Brooks and Brooks, *Original Analects,* p. 168.

3. Legge, *Works of Mencius,* 1:1:7, p. 143; ibid., 2:1:6, pp. 201–4; the quotation about becoming humane is from Bloom, "Fundamental Intuitions and Consensus Statements," p. 103.

4. Matthew 5:47, 5:38–42; Galatians 5:22–23.

5. Koran 4:41; 'Abdu'l-Bahá, *Promulgation of Universal Peace,* p. 387; 'Abdu'l-Bahá, *Selections from the Writings of 'Abdu'l-Bahá,* no. 138.

6. Bhagavad Gita 16.1, 17.20–21, 2.71, 12.13, 16.12.

7. Leviticus 19:10; Deuteronomy 15:7–8, 24:19–21; Proverbs 25:21.

8. Saraha's "Treasury of Songs," in Conze, *Buddhist Scriptures*, p. 180; "Sutta Nipata," Maghasutta, in Woodward, *Some Sayings of the Buddha*, p. 93; Nagarjuna, "Mahaprajnaparamitashastra," in Conze, *Buddhist Scriptures*, p. 32; Thurman, "Human Rights and Human Responsibilities," p. 96.

9. Analects 5.16, 13.9, 20.1.

10. Matthew 5:42; see Matthew 6:19–34, Luke 18:22; Galatians 5:22.

11. Koran 2:172, 76:8–9.

12. Bahá'u'lláh, *Epistle to the Son of the Wolf*, p. 93; Bahá'u'lláh, *Gleanings*, p. 265.

13. Bhagavad Gita 16.2.

14. Proverbs 31:8–9; Isaiah 1:17.

15. Luke 4:18; see Luke 4:16–21; Matthew 5:3, 5:5, 5:10.

16. Koran 4:77.

17. Bahá'u'lláh, in *Compilation of Compilations*, vol. 2, p. 379; Bahá'u'lláh, *Epistle to the Son of the Wolf*, p. 93.

18. Bhagavad Gita 16.2–3; Job 27:5–6; see Nagarjuna, "Mahaprajnaparamitashastra," in Conze, *Buddhist Scriptures*, p. 32; see Ashvaghosha, "Saundaranandakavya," in Conze, *Buddhist Scriptures*, p. 115; see Analects 15.27, 17.5; Analects 7.37.

19. Galatians 5:22, 6:9; Koran 42:41, 2:173; Bahá'u'lláh, Kitáb-i-Íqán, ¶213; 'Abdu'l-Bahá, *Some Answered Questions*, p. 79.

20. Bhagavad Gita 16.2; Leviticus 19:18; "Dhammapada," ch. 1, in Burtt, *Teachings of the Compassionate Buddha*, p. 52; Analects 8.5.

21. Matthew 5:39, 6:14–15, 7:1, 7:3; Romans 12:17–19.

22. Koran 5:49, 42:35, 42:41.

23. 'Abdu'l-Bahá, *Promulgation of Universal Peace*, p. 453; 'Abdu'l-Bahá, *Some Answered Questions*, pp. 271, 268.

24. Bhagavad Gita 16.2–3, 17.5; for an account of the principle of nonviolence in Hinduism and the Bhagavad Gita, see Edgerton, "Interpretation of the Bhagavad Gītā," pp. 185–86; Gandhi, *Autobiography*, p. 265.

25. Numbers 6:26; Psalms 34:15; Leviticus 19:34; for the injunction against murder, see Exodus 20:13; the quotation on not committing murder even at the cost of one's life is from Goodman, "The Individual and the Community," p. 44; for the quotation regarding might and power, see Zechariah 4:6.

26. Buddhaghosa, "Papancasudani," Sutta 9, in Conze, *Buddhist Scriptures*, p. 70; "Dhammapada," ch. 17, in Burtt, *Teachings of the Compassionate Buddha*, p. 64; see ibid.; on harmony and noncompetition, see Analects 1.12, 3.7; Analects 8.4, 17.22, 8.5.

27. Matthew 5:9; John 14:27; Matthew 26:52; Romans 12:16–18.

28. Koran 5:18, 5:35, 4:33.

29. Bahá'u'lláh, Kitáb-i-Aqdas, ¶19; 'Abdu'l-Bahá, *Will and Testament*, p. 13; 'Abdu'l-Bahá, *Paris Talks*, no. 6.7.

30. Bhagavad Gita 16.2, 17.15; Exodus 20:13; Leviticus 19:11; Proverbs 12:22; Buddhaghosa, "Papancasudani," Sutta 9, in Conze, *Buddhist Scriptures*, p. 70; "Dhammapada," ch. 17, in Burtt, *Teachings of the Compassionate Buddha*, p. 64; Analects 2.22.

31. Matthew 15:18–20; Koran 9:120, 4:111; Bahá'u'lláh, *Gleanings*, p. 297; Bahá'u'lláh, quoted in Shoghi Effendi, *Advent of Divine Justice*, p. 22.

32. Bhagavad Gita 16.4, 16.10; Numbers 30:3; "Bya chos" ("The Buddha's Law Among the Birds"), in Conze, *Buddhist Scriptures*, p. 89; Analects 2.13, 4.24.

33. Luke 16:10–12.

34. Koran 2:173; Bahá'u'lláh, *Gleanings*, p. 266; Bahá'u'lláh, *Epistle to the Son of the Wolf*, p. 93.

35. Bhagavad Gita 16.2, 16.4; Leviticus 19:16; Psalms 15:3.

36. "Dhammapada," ch. 17, in Burtt, *Teachings of the Compassionate Buddha*, pp. 64–65; "Dhammapada," ch. 10, in ibid., p. 60; Analects 6.29.

37. Matthew 18:15; James 3:6, 3:8–10; Romans 1:29–30.

38. Koran 49:12; Bahá'u'lláh, *Epistle to the Son of the Wolf*, pp. 93, 15; Bahá'u'lláh, Kitáb-i-Íqán, ¶214.

39. Bhagavad Gita 16.3, 16.10, 16.17; Proverbs 16:18-19.

40. "Dhammapada," ch. 18, in Burtt, *Teachings of the Compassionate Buddha*, p. 65.

41. On the love of learning, see Analects 1.14; Analects 2.17 (emphasis in original); the interpretation is from Brooks and Brooks, *Original Analects*, p. 112; Analects 12.21.

42. Matthew 18:1–4; Luke 18:14; Philippians 2:3.

43. Koran 23:1–4, 49:11; Bahá'u'lláh, *Tablets of Bahá'u'lláh*, p. 64; Bahá'u'lláh, *Hidden Words*, Persian, no. 44, Arabic, no. 27.

44. Bhagavad Gita 6.9, 2.47–48; on the meaning of indifference, see Bhagavad Gita 2.71.

45. Deuteronomy 16:18–20, 1:17; concerning the immorality of joining the majority if the majority is in the wrong, see Exodus 23:2; on the impartiality of judges, see Cohn, *Human Rights in Jewish Law*, p. 196; the quotation regarding equality before the law is from Exodus 12:49.

46. Jones, *Māhavastu*, p. 228; Jayatilleke, "The Principles of International Law in Buddhist Doctrine," p. 458.

47. On virtues, see Analects 4.11; Analects 4.10, 4.16, 2.14; for the interpretation of the passage in Analects 2.14, see Brooks and Brooks, *Original Analects*, p. 112; Analects 8.13, 13.22a, 15.19, 15.9; for the teachings of Mencius, see Legge, *Works of Mencius*, 6:1:10, p. 411.

48. Matthew 5:20; Matthew 10:37–38; on Jesus's teaching to love our enemies, see Matthew 5:43–48; Romans 2:11; see generally Romans 2:1–11.

49. Koran 4:134, 5:11; for commentary on the quoted passages from the Koran, see Rahman, *Major Themes of the Qur'ān*, pp. 42–43.

50. 'Abdu'l-Bahá, *Some Answered Questions*, p. 266; 'Abdu'l-Bahá, *Paris Talks*, no. 47.4; 'Abdu'l-Bahá, *Secret of Divine Civilization*, p. 39.

# 5 / The Equal Dignity
# of All Human Beings

The epigraph for chapter 5 is from "Dhammapada," ch. 26, in Burtt, *Teachings of the Compassionate Buddha,* p. 71.

1. Bhagavad Gita 9.29, 9.32, 5.18, 5.25.

2. Salgado, "Equality and Inequality," p. 64; Bhagavad Gita 5.19.

3. See Edgerton, "Interpretation of the Bhagavad Gītā," pp. 161–62 for a discussion of passages supporting the caste system; on interpretation of passages from the Gita to support equality, see Salgado, "Equality and Inequality," p. 65.

4. On the creation of human beings in God's image, see Genesis 1:27, 5:1; on the duty to treat others with kindness and love, see Kellner, "Jewish Ethics," pp. 84–85; Leviticus 24:22; Exodus 23:9; on rabbinical law, see Cohn, *Human Rights in Jewish Law,* pp. 159–66.

5. On the Buddhist teaching of equality, see Salgado, "Equality and Inequality," pp. 60–61 and Smith, *World's Religions,* p. 98; "Dhammapada," ch. 26, in Burtt, *Teachings of the Compassionate Buddha,* p. 71.

6. Analects 17.2a, 17.2b; Bloom, "Confucian Perspectives," p. 122; Analects 16.9 (emphasis in original); Bloom, "Confucian Perspectives," p. 121; Bloom, "Fundamental Intuitions and Consensus Statements," p. 109.

7. Matthew 25:31, 25:37–40.

8. On explanations for unequal treatment in the New Testament based on Greek thought, see Preston, "Christian Ethics," p. 102; Colossians 4:1.

9. See Koran 4:1; hadith quoted in Weeramantry, *Islamic Jurisprudence,* p. 133; on the teaching of equality in the Koran, see Rahman, *Major Themes of the Qur'ān,* pp. 45–46; Muḥammad's Farewell Sermon is from M. U. Akbar, *The Orations of Muhammad,* rev. ed. (Lahore: Muhammed Ashrof, 1966), quoted in Weeramantry, *Islamic Jurisprudence,* p. 173.

10. 'Abdu'l-Bahá, *Promulgation of Universal Peace,* p. 182; Bahá'u'lláh, quoted in Shoghi Effendi, *Advent of Divine Justice,* p. 31; 'Abdu'l-Bahá, quoted in ibid.

# 6 / Human Rights

The epigraph for chapter 6 is from 1 Corinthians 9:4, 9:11–12.

1. Ishay, "Introduction," p. xiv.

2. On virtues and duties in the Bhagavad Gita, see Bhagavad Gita 12.13–20, 16.1–3, 18.52–53; Bhagavad Gita 5.25.

3. For a review of the Ten Commandments, see Exodus 20; for a listing of some of the other commandments in the Hebrew scriptures, see Leviticus 19:10, 19:15–16, 19:34; for a list of the Noachide commandments, see Maimonides, "Treatise V: Laws Concerning Kings and Wars," pp. 230–31 and Fishbane, "The Image of the Human," pp. 25–26; the quotation by Michael Fishbane is from Fishbane, "The Image of the Human," p. 26.

4. On the relationship between rights and duties in the Hebrew scriptures, see Cohn, *Human Rights in Jewish Law*, pp. 1–23; on recognition that the duties in the Hebrew scriptures can give rise to rights, see Henkin, "Judaism and Human Rights," pp. 438–39; the quotations from the Hebrew scriptures are found in Proverbs 31:8–9 and Isaiah 61:1.

5. Buddhaghosa, "Papancasudani," Sutta 9, in Conze, *Buddhist Scriptures*, p. 70; Saraha's "Treasury of Songs," in Conze, *Buddhist Scriptures*, pp. 179–80.

6. For representative texts on selflessness or "no-self" in Buddhism, see Conze, *Buddhist Scriptures*, pp. 187–88; Unno, "Personal Rights and Contemporary Buddhism," p. 140.

7. On the duty of *ren* or *rŭn*, see Analects 17.5; for an attempt to relate the principles of the Analects to contemporary human rights concepts, see the essays collected in de Bary and Weiming, *Confucianism and Human Rights*; for the quotation from Irene Bloom, see Bloom, "Confucian Perspectives," p. 131; Analects 9.26; Brooks and Brooks, *Original Analects*, p. 106; on the freedom to claim rights in Confucianism, see Weiming, "Epilogue," p. 304.

8. Matthew 19:16–19.

9. On the implication of rights from universal duties in the Bible, but also a moral preference for not claiming rights out of a concern for others, see Harakas, "Human Rights: An Eastern Orthodox Perspective," pp. 18, 16; St. Paul's quotation is from 1 Corinthians 6:7.

10. 1 Corinthians 9:4, 9:11–12; John 18:23.

11. See Bulliet, "The Individual in Islamic Society."

12. Some of the relevant passages quoted from the Koran in chapter 4 are Koran 2:172–73 and 4:41.

13. 'Abdu'l-Bahá, *Promulgation of Universal Peace*, pp. 276–77, 182; 'Abdu'l-Bahá, *Secret of Divine Civilization*, p. 40.

14. 'Abdu'l-Bahá, *Secret of Divine Civilization*, p. 18.

# 7 / The Right to Life, Physical Security, and Subsistence

The epigraph for chapter 7 is from Analects 12.19 (emphasis in original).

1. Bhagavad Gita 16.14, 16.16.

2. On the absolute worth of every human life according to the Torah, see Fishbane, "The Image of the Human," pp. 17–20; Exodus 23:7; for a discussion of criminal procedural protections in the Torah, see Cohn, *Human Rights in Jewish Law*, pp. 208–16; on the eligibility of a case for the death penalty, see Fishbane, "The Image of the Human," p. 17, Numbers 35:30, and Deuteronomy 17:6, 19:15; the quotation on the guilt of children and their parents is from Ezekiel 18:20; on the concept of intergenerational guilt in the Torah, see Exodus 34:6–7.

3. Leviticus 24:19–20; for a discussion of this rule as a limitation on punishment based on proportionality to the injury, see Goodman, "The Individual and the Community," p. 21; on the prohibition of taking vengeance, see Leviticus 19:18; on the replacement of the rule of "an eye for an eye" with monetary compensation, see Cohn, *Human Rights in Jewish Law*, pp. 217–18.

4. On the Buddha's prohibition of killing and arms sales, see de Silva, "Buddhist Ethics," p. 66; on procedures for a fair trial, see Jayatilleke, "The Principles of International Law in Buddhist Doctrine," pp. 522–24.

5. Analects 8.4, 12.19 (emphasis in original), 13.11.

6. Matthew 19:18; John 18:23; Matthew 23:23; Langan, "The Individual and the Collectivity," p. 160.

7. See Koran 5:35.

8. Koran 4:122; on the principle of individual criminal responsibility in Islam, see al-Saleh, "The Right of the Individual to Personal Security in Islam," pp. 57–58; Sachedina, "Justifications for Violence in Islam," p. 140; on a preference for forgiveness, see Koran 5:49; al-Alfi, "Punishment in Islamic Criminal Law," p. 231.

9. Bahá'u'lláh, Kitáb-i-Aqdas, ¶19; 'Abdu'l-Bahá, *Some Answered Questions*, pp. 266–67; 'Abdu'l-Bahá, *Paris Talks*, no. 47.4.

10. On the duty to give, see Bhagavad Gita 17.20–21; Bhagavad Gita 12.4, 12.13, 16.1; on the recognition of entitlements of the poor in the Hebrew scriptures, see Polish, "Judaism and Human Rights," pp. 49–50; on the teachings of the Buddha, see "Sutta Nipata," Maghasutta, in Woodward, *Some Sayings of the Buddha*, p. 93; on the teachings of Confucius, see Analects 12.7, 5.16.

11. See Luke 18:22; 1 Corinthians 9:4; on the acknowledgment of economic rights in the Koran, see Rahman, *Major Themes of the Qur'ān*, pp. 39–42; Koran 51:15–19; on the law of *zakat*, see Rahman, *Major Themes of the Qur'ān*, pp. 40–42; see also Koran 9:60.

12. 'Abdu'l-Bahá, *Paris Talks*, no. 40.23; 'Abdu'l-Bahá, *Promulgation of Universal Peace*, p. 107.

# 8 / The Right to Freedom
# of Religion and Conscience

The epigraph for chapter 8 is from Koran 109:5.

1. Bhagavad Gita 4.39, 14.8; see Bhagavad Gita 5.4–6; Bhagavad Gita 7.17; for an analysis of the quoted passages from the Bhagavad Gita, see Edgerton, "Interpretation of the Bhagavad Gītā," pp. 164–71.

2. On tolerance of other religions in the Gita, see Edgerton, "Interpretation of the Bhagavad Gītā," pp. 179–82 and Minor, "The *Bhagavadgita* in Radhakrishnan's Apologetics," p. 169; Cox, "World Religions and Conflict Resolution," pp. 270–71.

3. On voluntary acceptance of the laws of the Hebrew scriptures, see Agus, "Religious Liberty in Judaism," p. 169; on the acquisition of learning, see Proverbs 1:1–6, 4:5–7; Job 7:11; on the principle of freedom of expression in the Hebrew scriptures, see Cohn, *Human Rights in Jewish Law*, pp. 107–28; on punishment for blasphemy and similar crimes, see Deuteronomy 13:2–12 and Leviticus 24:10–16; on punishment of actions, as opposed to beliefs, see Mendelssohn, "Freedom of Religion—Absolute and Inalienable," pp. 183–84; on the study of the Talmud as an exercise in independent investigation, see Goodman, "The Individual and the Community," p. 40.

4. The quotation on the Buddha seeking to break the grip of the *brahmins* is from Smith, *World's Religions*, p. 94; on the investigation of religious truth for oneself, see Abe, "Religious Tolerance and Human Rights," pp. 198–202; "Buddha's Farewell Address," Mahaparinibbana Suttanta, in Burtt, *Teachings of the Compassionate Buddha*, p. 49; "Anguttara Nikaya," 1.188, in Woodward, *Some Sayings of the Buddha*, p. 189; "Udanavarga," 9 Shilavarga, in Conze, *Buddhist Scriptures*, p. 86; on open-mindedness toward other religions, see Abe, "Religious Tolerance and Human Rights," pp. 198–202; Saraha's "Treasury of Songs," in Conze, *Buddhist Scriptures*, p. 176.

5. Analects 7.8, 9.26.

6. Ibid., 2.15, 19.6.

7. On freedom of conscience in the New Testament, see Tutu, "Religious Human Rights and the Bible," p. 66; on Jesus's call to individuals to repent, see Langan, "The Individual and the Collectivity," p. 159; John 7:17, 4:9.

8. Acts 17:22, 17:26–28; Romans 2:15.

9. Romans 2:9, 2:11; see generally Romans 2:1–11; Hebrews 1:1–2.

10. On the teaching in the Koran that faith is personal, see Sachedina, "Freedom of Conscience and Religion in the Qur'an," p. 76; Koran 2:257, 10:99–100, 18:28; on the emphasis on free choice in the Koran, see Rahman, *Major Themes of the Qur'ān*, p. 20.

11. Koran 3:84; on hadiths prescribing the death penalty for apostasy, see Khadduri, *War and Peace in the Law of Islam*, pp. 150–51; on the absence of Koranic references to earthly punishment for apostasy, see Hassan, "Religious Human Rights and the Qur'an," p. 91.

12. On the *umma*, see Koran 3:100; Koran 3:78, 46:8; Rahman, *Major Themes of the Qur'ān*, p. 83.

13. Koran 5:50, 2:59, 3:57.

14. Ibid., 5:51; see Hamidullah, *Muslim Conduct of State*, pp. 141–43.

15. Koran 109:5, 5:3, 88:21–22; on the tolerance of the early Muslim community toward Jews and Christians, see Smith, *World's Religions*, pp. 255–57.

16. On the Bahá'í writings' exhortation to search independently for the truth, see Hatcher and Martin, *Bahá'í Faith*, pp. 86–87; 'Abdu'l-Bahá, *Paris Talks*, no. 40.18; on the relationship between faith and reason, see Hatcher and Martin, *Bahá'í Faith*, pp. xv–xvi; 'Abdu'l-Bahá, *Promulgation of Universal Peace*, p. 197.

17. Bahá'u'lláh, *Tablets of Bahá'u'lláh*, p. 22; 'Abdu'l-Bahá, *Promulgation of Universal Peace*, p. 394.

# 9 / The Status of Women

The epigraph for chapter 9 is from *Compilation of Compilations*, vol. 2, p. 379.

1. Bhagavad Gita 9.32.

2. Genesis 2:18, 2:21; see Genesis 3:1–7; Genesis 3:16.

3. On discrimination against women in rabbinical law, see Cohn, *Human Rights in Jewish Law*, pp. 167–77; for a fuller treatment of the status of women in the Hebrew scriptures and in Judaism, see Carmody, "Judaism."

4. Genesis 1:27, 2:24.

5. For an analysis of Chapter 31 of Proverbs and other women-affirming stories and passages, see Goodman, "The Individual and the Community," pp. 29–31; Proverbs 7:4.

6. On discrimination against women, see Barnes, "Buddhism," pp. 106–9, 131.

7. On the Buddha's admission of women to an order of monks, see Salgado, "Equality and Inequality," pp. 61–64; "Samyutta Nikāya," 1.3.3, in Barnes, "Buddhism," p. 106; "Samyutta Nikāya," 3.2.6, in Salgado, "Equality and Inequality," p. 61.

8. Analects 17.23; on the subordinate role of women in Confucianism, see Kelleher, "Confucianism."

9. On a woman being able to achieve the status of "noble person," see Bloom, "Confucian Perspectives," pp. 121–22, 148–49 n10; Brooks and Brooks, *Original Analects*, p. 166; see also Analects 6.28.

10. On the prohibition of women participating in church discussions, see 1 Corinthians 14:33–35; the quotation from St. Paul is from Colossians 3:18; the quotation from St. Peter is from 1 Peter 3:1–2, 3:6.

11. On the interpretation of certain passages as reflecting patriarchal assumptions of the era, see McDonald, *Biblical Interpretation and Christian Ethics*, pp. 197–98; for a more comprehensive treatment of the role of women in Christian scripture and practice, see Ruether, "Christianity"; the quotations from St. Paul are from 1 Corinthians 11:11 and Galatians 3:28; see Luke 8:1–3 for a mention of women accompanying Jesus;

McDonald, *Biblical Interpretation and Christian Ethics*, p. 197.

12. Koran 2:227, 4:38; on inheritance rules, see Koran 4:11–14; on the subjugation of women in Islamic law and practice, see Mayer, *Islam and Human Rights*, pp. 97–130.

13. Mayer, *Islam and Human Rights*, pp. 97–98.

14. Smith, "Islam," pp. 242–43; Koran 4:123, 4:36; Muḥammad's Farewell Sermon is from S.A. Khan, *Anecdotes from Islam*, rev. ed. (Lahore: Muhammed Ashrof, 1960), quoted in Weeramantry, *Islamic Jurisprudence*, p. 172.

15. On men having greater obligations at the time of the Koran's revelation, see Smith, "Islam," pp. 239–40; on the discriminatory rules of Islam evolving from the opinions of male jurists or patriarchal traditions, see Mayer, *Islam and Human Rights*, pp. 98, 127–28.

16. Bahá'u'lláh, in *Compilation of Compilations*, vol. 2, p. 379; 'Abdu'l-Bahá, *Promulgation of Universal Peace*, pp. 375, 135.

17. 'Abdu'l-Bahá, *Promulgation of Universal Peace*, p. 168.

# 10 / A Trust Theory of Government and Limited State Sovereignty

The epigraph for chapter 10 is from Analects 6.22.

1. Bhagavad Gita 16.14–15, 16.1–2, 16.24.

2. Psalms 72:1–2, 72:4, 72:12–14.

3. Deuteronomy 17:18–20, 16:18–19; on persons being treated as equal before the law, see Exodus 12:49.

4. Isaiah 40:23; Bentwich, *Religious Foundations of Internationalism*, p. 61; Rosenne, "The Influence of Judaism," p. 149.

5. de Silva, "Buddhist Ethics," p. 65; on the responsibility of kings, see Jayatilleke, "The Principles of International Law in Buddhist Doctrine," pp. 528–33; ibid., pp. 472, 478.

6. Analects 12.7; on the primary factor in judging leaders, see Analects 13.16, 5.16, 13.9; Analects 1.5, 6.22.

7. Analects 13.13, 2.3.

8. Legge, *Works of Mencius*, 7:2:14, p. 483 (emphasis in original).

9. Acts 5:29; Matthew 20:25–28; 1 Corinthians 15:24.

10. Kooijmans, "Protestantism and the Development of International Law," p. 98.

11. Koran 3:73, 5:20, 4:61, 38:25.

12. Ibid., 3:100, 3:109–10; hadith from Ahmad Ibrahim, "The Concept of Justice in Islam," *Malayan Law Journal* 2 (1985), quoted in Weeramantry, *Islamic Jurisprudence*, p. 116.

13. Khadduri, *War and Peace in the Law of Islam*, p. 12; on the authority of caliphs, see ibid., pp. 14–18; Weeramantry, *Islamic Jurisprudence*, p. 125.

14. Bahá'u'lláh, *Tablets of Bahá'u'lláh*, p. 164; Bahá'u'lláh, Summons of the Lord of Hosts, "Súriy-i-Haykal," ¶174.

15. Bahá'u'lláh, Summons of the Lord of Hosts, "Súriy-i-Mulúk," ¶20–21; 'Abdu'l-Bahá, *Secret of Divine Civilization*, p. 115.

16. Shoghi Effendi, *World Order of Bahá'u'lláh*, p. 202.

# 11 / Open-Minded Consultation

The epigraph for chapter 11 is from Bahá'u'lláh, *Tablets of Bahá'u'lláh*, p. 168.

1. Bhagavad Gita 16.4, 16.2.

2. Deuteronomy 1:17; Proverbs 15:22; Ecclesiastes 12:9; Zechariah 8:16; Genesis 1:26; Goodman, "The Individual and the Community," p. 42; on the consent of the council of rabbis before launching a war, see Broyde, "Fighting the War and the Peace," pp. 23–24 n26; on the requirement that judges consult with one another, see Cohn, *Human Rights in Jewish Law*, pp. 205–6.

3. Cox, "World Religions and Conflict Resolution," p. 272; "Sutta Nipata," in Conze, *Buddhist Scriptures*, p. 77; on the Buddha's opposition to religious dissension, see the passages from "Sutta Nipata" reproduced in Burtt, *Teachings of the Compassionate Buddha*, pp. 36–39; "Dhammapada," ch. 17, in ibid., p. 64; the story of the blind men and the elephant appears in "Udana," 6.4, in Woodward, *Some Sayings of the Buddha*, pp. 190–92.

4. Analects 4.17.

5. Ibid., 7.22, 15.8, 13.23, 15.28.

6. See Legge, *Works of Mencius*, 1:2:7, pp. 165–66; Cheng, "Transforming Confucian Virtues into Human Rights," pp. 150–51.

7. 1 Corinthians 14:26, 14:29–31; on consultation among Jesus's disciples, see Acts 15; Yoder, "On Not Being in Charge," p. 82.

8. Koran 3:153; on *shúrá*, see also Koran 42:36 and Rahman, *Major Themes of the Qur'án*, pp. 43–44; hadith quoted in Weeramantry, *Islamic Jurisprudence*, p. 26; hadith quoted in ibid., p. 92; for more on Muḥammad's consultation with his followers and on shúrá, see ibid., pp. 123–24.

9. Weeramantry, *Islamic Jurisprudence*, p. 124; Hassan, "On Human Rights and the Qur'anic Perspective," p. 60.

10. Bahá'u'lláh, *Tablets of Bahá'u'lláh*, p. 168; 'Abdu'l-Bahá, *Promulgation of Universal Peace*, pp. 72–73.

# 12 / Respect for
# Governments and Law

The epigraph for chapter 12 is from Koran 4:62.

1. Bhagavad Gita 16.23–24; one modern interpreter who found a warrant in the Bhagavad Gita for questioning societal authorities is Radhakrishnan. See Minor, "The *Bhagavadgita* in Radhakrishnan's Apologetics," p. 170.

2. Jeremiah 29:7; Ecclesiastes 8:2, 8:5; Deuteronomy 17:11.

3. See Exodus 1:15–22; Maimonides, "Treatise V: Laws Concerning Kings and Wars," pp. 213–14; Gendler, "The Pursuit of Peace," p. 34.

4. Jayatilleke, "The Principles of International Law in Buddhist Doctrine," pp. 478, 506; on a right of rebellion but a moral preference for nonviolent resistance, see ibid., pp. 527–28.

5. Analects 4.11, 13.15 (emphasis in original), 11.22.

6. On a right to revolt against tyranny as a last resort, see Chen, "The Confucian View of World Order," pp. 37–38; de Bary, "Introduction," p. 8; see Legge, *Works of Mencius*, 1:2:8, p. 167; ibid., 5:2:9, p. 392; Bloom, "Confucian Perspectives," p. 144.

7. Matthew 22:17, 22:21.

8. Romans 13:1–4; on various interpretations of Romans 13:1–6, see Bainton, *Christian Attitudes Toward War and Peace*, pp. 59–61.

9. Langan, "The Individual and the Collectivity," p. 162.

10. Acts 5:29; Matthew 23:23; Küng, "Towards a World Ethic of World Religions," p. 117.

11. On the interpretation of Romans 13:1–4 as justifying obedience only to just laws and rulers, see Yoder, *Politics of Jesus*, pp. 208–9 and Ramsey, *Basic Christian Ethics*, p. 386; Langan, "The Individual and the Collectivity," p. 163.

12. Koran 4:62.

13. On the Islamic view of obedience to government as necessary, see Sachedina, "Justifications for Violence in Islam," p. 149; hadith quoted in Hamidullah, *Muslim Conduct of State*, p. 186; see ibid., pp. 128, 130.

14. For more on rebellion under Islamic law, see Abou El Fadl, *Rebellion and Violence in Islamic Law*; Koran 49:9, 26:150–52; hadith quoted in Sachedina, "Justifications for Violence in Islam," p. 136.

15. Bahá'u'lláh, *Tablets of Bahá'u'lláh*, pp. 22–23; see extract from a letter written on behalf of Shoghi Effendi to an individual Bahá'í dated December 21, 1948, reprinted in Hornby, *Lights of Guidance*, no. 1453.

16. 'Abdu'l-Bahá, *Promulgation of Universal Peace*, p. 224.

# 13 / Peace, Justice, and Respect for Treaties and International Law

1. On the kings of India being subject to dharma, see Nanda, "International Law in Ancient Hindu India," pp. 51–52; on the Code of Manu, see Bühler, *Laws of Manu*, ch. 7, ¶198 at p. 248.

2. 1 Chronicles 28:2–3.

3. On the Buddhist promotion of peace, see Ashvaghosha, "Buddhacarita," in Conze, *Buddhist Scriptures*, p. 52; on the prohibition of killing and arms selling and the "futility of warfare," see de Silva, "Buddhist Ethics," p. 66; Jones, *Mahāvastu*, p. 229.

4. Analects 13.29.

5. Ephesians 2:14–17.

6. Koran 49:13, 5:53.

7. Bahá'u'lláh, Summons of the Lord of Hosts, "Súrih-i-Haykal," ¶42; see ibid., ¶42, 182.

8. Bhagavad Gita 16.1–2; on the duty to use force, see the discussion in chapter 14.

9. Bentwich, *Religious Foundations of Internationalism*, p. 66; Goodman, "Pacifism and Nonviolence," pp. 67–68; Isaiah 32:17.

10. Carus, *Gospel of Buddha*, p. 148; see Analects 14.34.

11. Bainton, *Christian Attitudes Toward War and Peace*, pp. 54–55; Matthew 23:23.

12. Koran 49:9; Sachedina, "Justifications for Violence in Islam," p. 155.

13. 'Abdu'l-Bahá, *Compilation of Compilations*, vol. 2, p. 165.

14. On the story of the Gibeonites, see Joshua 9 and the analysis in Broyde, "Fighting the War and the Peace," pp. 15–17; Joshua 9:15, 9:19; Broyde, "Fighting the War and the Peace," p. 16.

15. Koran 9:4, 16:93–94; on the sanctity of treaties under Islamic law, see Weeramantry, *Islamic Jurisprudence*, pp. 140–41; on the principle that "treaties are to be observed," see Boisard, "On the Probable Influence of Islam," pp. 441–42.

16. 'Abdu'l-Bahá, *Promulgation of Universal Peace*, p. 344; on a collective security treaty, see Bahá'u'lláh, Summons of the Lord of Hosts, "Súrih-i-Haykal," ¶182 and 'Abdu'l-Bahá, *Secret of Divine Civilization*, pp. 64–65.

17. Micah 4:2–3; see also Isaiah 2:3–4; Nussbaum, *Concise History of the Law of Nations*, pp. 9–10; Gordis, "The Vision of Micah," pp. 282–83, 287.

18. Jayatilleke, "The Principles of International Law in Buddhist Doctrine," pp. 540, 541; on a world statesman, see generally pp. 452, 493, 538–41.

19. See Acts 17:27–28.

20. Koran 4:62; see Koran 49:9; on conciliation and arbitration in Islamic law and practice, see Rahman, *Major Themes of the Qur'ān*, p. 44; Hamidullah, *Muslim Conduct of State*, pp. 152–56.

21. Shoghi Effendi, *World Order of Bahá'u'lláh*, p. 203; see ibid., pp. 202–4 and 'Abdu'l-Bahá, *Selections from the Writings of 'Abdu'l-Bahá*, no. 227.

# 14 / The Legitimate Use of Force

The epigraph for chapter 14 is from Carus, *Gospel of Buddha*, p. 148.

1. Bhagavad Gita 2.18; on the ethical contradictions in the Bhagavad Gita involving *ahimsā* and the Gita's use to justify both violence and nonviolence, see Sharma, *The Hindu Gītā*, pp. xiv–xv.

2. On Edgerton's views, see Edgerton, "Interpretation of the Bhagavad Gītā," pp. 105–10, 185–86; on Gandhi's interpretation, see Jordens, "Gandhi and the *Bhagavadgita*," p. 98; on the Gita condemning those who take pride in slaying others, see Bhagavad Gita 16.14, 16.16; A. R. Nikhilananda, *Teachings of the Bhagawad Gita*, quoted in Sastry, "Hinduism and International Law," p. 529.

3. For an example of a scholarly view that Judaism is fundamentally pacifist, see Goodman, "Pacifism and Nonviolence," p. 67; Ecclesiastes 3:8; for examples of instructions to wage war against the Canaanite nations and the Amalekites, see Deuteronomy 7:1–5, 20:15–18, 25:17–19; on the obligatory nature of certain wars, see Maimonides, "Treatise V: Laws Concerning Kings and Wars," p. 217; on the justification for wars against the seven nations disappearing, see Cohn, *Human Rights in Jewish Law*, p. 155 and Maimonides, "Treatise V: Laws Concerning Kings and Wars," p. 217.

4. On the requirement of consent of the Sanhedrin, see Maimonides, "Treatise V: Laws Concerning Kings and Wars," p. 217; Deuteronomy 20:12–14; Oppenheim, *International Law*, pp. 46–47.

5. Deuteronomy 20:10; see Deuteronomy 20:15; Maimonides, "Treatise V: Laws Concerning Kings and Wars," p. 220; see generally ibid., pp. 220–21.

6. Carus, *Gospel of Buddha*, p. 148; on a right of self-defense but a preference for nonviolent methods of conflict resolution, see Jayatilleke, "The Principles of International Law in Buddhist Doctrine," pp. 549–51; Bentwich, *Religious Foundations of Internationalism*, p. 187.

7. Analects 13.29; on the condemnation of wars in the "Spring and Autumn" period, see Chen, "The Confucian View of World Order," pp. 33–34; Legge, *Works of Mencius*, 7:2:4, p. 479; ibid., 7:2:2, p. 478; on self-defense, see Chen, "The Confucian View of World Order," pp. 34–35; Legge, *Works of Mencius*, 1:2:13, p. 174.

8. Romans 12:18; Luke 22:36–38; Matthew 10:34; Matthew 8:5–13; Luke 3:14.

9. Bainton, *Christian Attitudes Toward War and Peace*, p. 53; on Jesus's overturning of the tables of the money changers, see John 2:13–15.

10. For examples of the view that Jesus taught nonviolence, see Yoder, "On Not Being in Charge" and Wink, "Beyond Just War and Pacifism"; on the views of Reinhold Niebuhr, see Niebuhr, "Why the Christian Church Is Not Pacifist"; St. Thomas Aquinas, *The Summa of Theology, Part II, Second Part*, Qu. 40, reprinted in Sigmund, *St. Thomas Aquinas on Politics and Ethics*, pp. 64–65.

11. Wink, "Beyond Just War and Pacifism," p. 111 (emphasis in original); ibid., pp. 116–17.

12. On ambiguity in the Koran's verses dealing with jihad, see Peters, *Jihad in Classical and Modern Islam*, p. 2; Koran 5:3, 2:187, 4:92, 2:188.

13. Koran 47:4–5, 9:29.

14. Peters, *Jihad in Classical and Modern Islam*, p. 2.

15. 'Abdu'l-Bahá, *Secret of Divine Civilization*, pp. 70–71.

16. Koran 49:9.

17. Bahá'u'lláh, *Tablets of Bahá'u'lláh*, p. 165.

18. Nussbaum, *Concise History of the Law of Nations*, p. 10; on the Code of Manu, see Bühler, *The Laws of Manu*, ch. 7, ¶90–93 at pp. 230–31.

19. See Deuteronomy 20:19–20; Maimonides, "Treatise V: Laws Concerning Kings and Wars," p. 222; see ibid., pp. 222–23; Nussbaum, *Concise History of the Law of Nations*, p. 9; on the requirement that civilians be allowed to escape before an attack, see Maimonides, "Treatise V: Laws Concerning Kings and Wars," pp. 221–22 and Broyde, "Fighting the War and the Peace," pp. 10–11.

20. Carus, *Gospel of Buddha*, p. 149; Analects 13.11; see Analects 13.29.

21. See St. Augustine, *The Political Writings of St. Augustine*, p. 183; on the principle of double effect, see St. Thomas Aquinas, *The Summa of Theology, Part II, Second Part*, Qu. 64, reprinted in Sigmund, *St. Thomas Aquinas on Politics and Ethics*, p. 70; on Christian just war theory, see Wink, "Beyond Just War and Pacifism," pp. 111–12.

22. On Islamic rules on the humane conduct of war, see generally Weeramantry, *Islamic Jurisprudence*, pp. 134–38; Hamidullah, *Muslim Conduct of State*, pp. 202–32, 275; Koran 2:187, 76:8, 47:4–5, 5:3; regarding hadiths in which Muḥammad prohibited the killing of women and children, see the two hadiths quoted in Peters, *Jihad in Classical and Modern Islam*, p. 13.

23. Nussbaum, *Concise History of the Law of Nations*, p. 28; Bentwich, *Religious Foundations of Internationalism*, p. 169 (emphasis in original).

24. See 'Abdu'l-Bahá, *Selections from the Writings of 'Abdu'l-Bahá*, no. 81.1 and 'Abdu'l-Bahá, *Paris Talks*, nos. 6.1–6; Bahá'u'lláh, *Tablets of Bahá'u'lláh*, p. 23.

25. 'Abdu'l-Bahá, *Secret of Divine Civilization*, p. 65.

# 15 / Intervention to Rescue Human Rights Victims

1. Bhagavad Gita 16.1–2.
2. Leviticus 19:16; see Exodus 2:11–12; Psalms 82:3–4, 72:12; Job 29:16; Proverbs 24:11–12.
3. Maimonides, "Treatise V: Murder and the Preservation of Life," p. 198 (emphasis in original).
4. On saving a human life, see Goodman, "The Individual and the Community," p. 43; Maimonides, "Treatise V: Murder and the Preservation of Life," p. 196.
5. See Broyde, "Fighting the War and the Peace," pp. 2–7; ibid., p. 7.
6. Carus, *Gospel of Buddha*, p. 148.
7. Chen, "The Confucian View of World Order," p. 35; for the story of Qi and Yan, see Legge, *Works of Mencius*, 1:2:10–11, pp. 169–72; correspondence between the author and Irene Bloom dated July 13–14, 1998 (emphasis in original).
8. On the stoning of an adulteress, see John 8:1–11; for a work advocating nonviolent intervention based on John 8:1–11 and Jesus's teachings, see Aukerman, "The Scandal of Defenselessness," pp. 75–77.
9. Ramsey, *The Just War*, p. 501 (emphasis in original); on the endorsement of humanitarian intervention by Christian just war theorists, see Himes, "Just War, Pacifism and Humanitarian Intervention" (applying Catholic just war doctrine to humanitarian intervention).
10. Koran 4:77; Sinaceur, "Islamic Tradition and Human Rights," p. 215; hadith from the "Sahih Bukhari," quoted in Nagler, "Is There a Tradition of Nonviolence in Islam?," p. 165; for further reading on an Islamic ethic of humanitarian intervention, see Hashmi, "Is There an Islamic Ethic of Humanitarian Intervention?"
11. Matthew 5:39.
12. 'Abdu'l-Bahá, *Some Answered Questions*, pp. 270–71.
13. Bahá'u'lláh, *Epistle to the Son of the Wolf*, p. 93.
14. Bahá'u'lláh, *Tablets of Bahá'u'lláh*, p. 165.

# 16 / Optimism and Pragmatism

The epigraph for chapter 16 is from Matthew 5:48.
1. On the international relations theory counterparts of the three philosophical views described in the text, see Wight, *International Theory*, pp. 25–29. Wight refers to "revolutionists," "realists," and "rationalists" to describe adherents to optimism, pessimism, and pragmatism respectively.

2. Compare Bhagavad Gita 16.1–5 with 2.18; Leviticus 19:2; Ecclesiastes 8:5.

3. Ashvaghosha, "Buddhacarita," in Conze, *Buddhist Scriptures*, p. 62; Carus, *Gospel of Buddha*, p. 148; Jayatilleke, "The Principles of International Law in Buddhist Doctrine," pp. 496, 535.

4. Analects 7.30, 15.15–16 (emphasis in original), 12.11.

5. Matthew 5:48; Romans 12:2; Niebuhr, "Optimism, Pessimism and Religious Faith - II," p. 200.

6. Rahman, *Major Themes of the Qur'ān*, p. 30; Koran 4:62.

7. 'Abdu'l-Bahá, *Promulgation of Universal Peace*, p. 155; Bahá'u'lláh, *Tablets of Bahá'u'lláh*, p. 171; Bahá'u'lláh, quoted in Shoghi Effendi, *God Passes By*, p. 194.

# 17 / The Prospects for a Global Ethic

The epigraph for chapter 17 is from Bahá'u'lláh, *Tablets of Bahá'u'lláh*, pp. 63–64.

1. The 1970 Kyoto Declaration of the First Assembly of the World Conference on Religion and Peace, October 1970, reprinted in Braybrooke, *Stepping Stones to a Global Ethic*, pp. 42–43; for the text of the *Declaration Toward a Global Ethic*, see Küng and Kuschel, *A Global Ethic*, pp. 11–39.

2. See Smith, *World's Religions*, pp. 386–89; Huntington, *Clash of Civilizations*, p 320.

3. Falk, "Panel #1 Presentation," p. 23; Johnston, "Looking Ahead," pp. 332–33.

4. Allport, *Nature of Prejudice*, p. 455; see ibid., pp. 444–57, especially p. 455

5. 'Abdu'l-Bahá, *Paris Talks*, no. 42.11

# Bibliography

# Works of Bahá'u'lláh

*Epistle to the Son of the Wolf*. Translated by Shoghi Effendi. 1st ps ed. Wilmette, IL: Bahá'í Publishing Trust, 1988.

*Gleanings from the Writings of Bahá'u'lláh*. 1st ps ed. Translated by Shoghi Effendi. Wilmette, IL: Bahá'í Publishing Trust, 1983.

*The Hidden Words*. Translated by Shoghi Effendi. Wilmette, IL: Bahá'í Publishing, 2002.

*The Kitáb-i-Aqdas: The Most Holy Book*. 1st ps ed. Wilmette, IL: Bahá'í Publishing Trust, 1993.

*The Kitáb-i-Íqán: The Book of Certitude*. Translated by Shoghi Effendi. Wilmette, IL: Bahá'í Publishing, 2003.

*The Summons of the Lord of Hosts: Tablets of Bahá'u'lláh*. Haifa, Israel: Bahá'í World Centre, 2002.

*Tablets of Bahá'u'lláh revealed after the Kitáb-i-Aqdas*. Compiled by the Research Department of the Universal House of Justice. Translated by Habib Taherzadeh et al. 1st ps ed. Wilmette, IL: Bahá'í Publishing Trust, 1988.

# Works of 'Abdu'l-Bahá

*Paris Talks: Addresses Given by 'Abdu'l-Bahá in Paris in 1911*. 12th ed. London: Bahá'í Publishing Trust, 1995.

*The Promulgation of Universal Peace: Talks Delivered by 'Abdu'l-Bahá During His Visit to the United States and Canada in 1912*. 2nd ed. Compiled by Howard MacNutt. Wilmette, IL: Bahá'í Publishing Trust, 1982.

*The Secret of Divine Civilization*. 1st ps ed. Translated by Marzieh Gail and Ali-Kuli Khan. Wilmette, IL: Bahá'í Publishing Trust, 1990.

*Selections from the Writings of 'Abdu'l-Bahá*. Compiled by the Research Department of the Universal House of Justice. Translated by a committee at the Bahá'í World Center and by Marzieh Gail. Wilmette, IL: Bahá'í Publishing Trust, 1997.

*Some Answered Questions*. Compiled and translated by Laura Clifford Barney. 1st ps ed. Wilmette, IL: Bahá'í Publishing Trust, 1984.

*Will and Testament of 'Abdu'l-Bahá*. Wilmette, IL: Bahá'í Publishing Trust, 1944.

# Works of Shoghi Effendi

*The Advent of Divine Justice.* 3rd rev. ed. Wilmette, IL: Bahá'í Publishing Trust, 1969.
*God Passes By.* New ed. Wilmette, IL: Bahá'í Publishing Trust, 1974.
*The World Order of Bahá'u'lláh: Selected Letters.* 1st ps ed. Wilmette, IL: Bahá'í Publishing Trust, 1991.

# Other Works

Abe, Masao. "Religious Tolerance and Human Rights: A Buddhist Perspective." In *Religious Liberty and Human Rights in Nations and in Religions*, edited by Leonard Swidler, pp. 193–211. Philadelphia: Ecumenical Press, 1986.

Abou El Fadl, Khaled. *Rebellion and Violence in Islamic Law.* Cambridge: Cambridge University Press, 2001.

Agus, Jacob B. "Religious Liberty in Judaism." In *Religious Liberty and Human Rights in Nations and in Religions*, edited by Leonard Swidler, pp. 167–74. Philadelphia: Ecumenical Press, 1986.

al-Alfi, Ahmad Abd al-Aziz. "Punishment in Islamic Criminal Law." In *The Islamic Criminal Justice System*, edited by M. Cherif Bassiouni, pp. 227–36. London: Oceana, 1982.

Allport, Gordon W. *The Nature of Prejudice.* Twenty-fifth anniversary edition. Reading, MA: Addison-Wesley, 1979.

Aquinas, St. Thomas. *The Summa of Theology, Part II, Second Part.* Reprinted in part in *St. Thomas Aquinas on Politics and Ethics: A New Translation, Backgrounds, Interpretations*, translated and edited by Paul E. Sigmund, pp. 61–80. New York: W. W. Norton, 1988.

Arberry, A. J., trans. *The Koran Interpreted.* New York: Simon & Schuster, 1955.

Augustine, St. *The Political Writings of St. Augustine.* Edited by Henry Paolucci. Washington, DC: Regnery Gateway, 1962.

Aukerman, Dale. "The Scandal of Defenselessness." In John Howard Yoder et al., *What Would You Do? A Serious Answer to a Standard Question*, pp. 75–77. Scottdale, PA: Herald Press, 1983.

Bainton, Roland H. *Christian Attitudes Toward War and Peace: A Historical Survey and Critical Re-evaluation.* New York: Abingdon, 1960.

Barnes, Nancy Schuster. "Buddhism." In *Women in World Religions*, edited by Arvind Sharma, pp. 105–33. Albany: State University of New York Press, 1987.

Bentwich, Norman. *The Religious Foundations of Internationalism: A Study in International Relations through the Ages.* 2nd ed. New York: Bloch Publishing, 1959.

Bloom, Irene. "Confucian Perspectives on the Individual and the Collectivity." In *Reli-*

*gious Diversity and Human Rights*, edited by Irene Bloom, J. Paul Martin, and Wayne L. Proudfoot, pp. 114–51. New York: Columbia University Press, 1996.

———. "Fundamental Intuitions and Consensus Statements: Mencian Confucianism and Human Rights." In *Confucianism and Human Rights*, edited by Wm. Theodore de Bary and Tu Weiming, pp. 94–116. New York: Columbia University Press, 1998.

Boisard, Marcel A. "On the Probable Influence of Islam on Western Public and International Law." *International Journal of Middle East Studies* 11 (1980): 429–50.

Braybrooke, Marcus. *Stepping Stones to a Global Ethic*. London: SCM Press, 1992.

Brooks, E. Bruce, and A. Taeko Brooks, trans. *The Original Analects: Sayings of Confucius and His Successors*. New York: Columbia University Press, 1998.

Broyde, Michael J. "Fighting the War and the Peace: Battlefield Ethics, Peace Talks, Treaties, and Pacifism in the Jewish Tradition." In *War and Its Discontents: Pacifism and Quietism in the Abrahamic Traditions*, edited by J. Patout Burns, pp. 1–30. Washington, DC: Georgetown University Press, 1996.

Bühler, G., trans. *The Laws of Manu*. Delhi: Motilal Banarsidass, 1964.

Bulliet, Richard W. "The Individual in Islamic Society." In *Religious Diversity and Human Rights*, edited by Irene Bloom, J. Paul Martin, and Wayne L. Proudfoot, pp. 175–91. New York: Columbia University Press, 1996.

Burtt, E. A., ed. *The Teachings of the Compassionate Buddha*. New York: Penguin Putnam, 1982.

Carmody, Denise L. "Judaism." In *Women in World Religions*, edited by Arvind Sharma, pp. 183–206. Albany: State University of New York Press, 1987.

Cartwright, Michael G. "Biblical Argument in International Ethics." In *Traditions of International Ethics*, edited by Terry Nardin and David R. Mapel, pp. 270–96. Cambridge: Cambridge University Press, 1992.

Carus, Paul, comp. *The Gospel of Buddha*. Chicago: Open Court, 1915.

Chen, Frederick Tse-Shyang. "The Confucian View of World Order." In *Religion and International Law*, edited by Mark W. Janis and Carolyn Evans, pp. 27–49. The Hague: Martinus Nijhoff, 1999.

Cheng, Chung-ying. "Transforming Confucian Virtues into Human Rights: A Study of Human Agency and Potency in Confucian Ethics." In *Confucianism and Human Rights*, edited by Wm. Theodore de Bary and Tu Weiming, pp. 142–53. New York: Columbia University Press, 1998.

Cohn, Haim H. *Human Rights in Jewish Law*. New York: KTAV Publishing House, 1984.

*Compilation of Compilations: Prepared by the Universal House of Justice, 1963–1990*. Vol. 2. Maryborough, Victoria: Bahá'í Publications Australia, 1991.

Conze, Edward. *Buddhism: Its Essence and Development*. New York: Harper & Row, 1959.

———, trans. *Buddhist Scriptures*. London: Penguin Books, 1959.

Cox, Harvey, et al. "World Religions and Conflict Resolution." In *Religion, The Missing Dimension of Statecraft*, edited by Douglas Johnston and Cynthia Sampson, pp. 266–82. New York: Oxford University Press, 1994.

Damrosch, Lori Fisler, and Bernard H. Oxman et al. "Agora: Future Implications of the

Iraq Conflict." *American Journal of International Law* 97 (2003): 553–642.

de Bary, Wm. Theodore. "Introduction." In *Confucianism and Human Rights*, edited by Wm. Theodore de Bary and Tu Weiming, pp. 1–26. New York: Columbia University Press, 1998.

de Bary, Wm. Theodore, and Tu Weiming, eds. *Confucianism and Human Rights*. New York: Columbia University Press, 1998.

de Silva, Padmasiri. "Buddhist Ethics." In *A Companion to Ethics*, edited by Peter Singer, pp. 58–68. Oxford: Blackwell, 1993.

———. "The Concept of Equality in the Theravāda Buddhist Tradition." In *Equality and the Religious Traditions of Asia*, edited by R. Siriwardena, pp. 74–97. New York: St. Martins Press, 1987.

Edgerton, Franklin. "Interpretation of the Bhagavad Gītā." In *The Bhagavad Gītā*, translated and interpreted by Franklin Edgerton, pp. 103–202. Cambridge: Harvard University Press, 1972.

———, trans. *The Bhagavad Gītā*. Cambridge: Harvard University Press, 1972.

Falk, Richard. "Panel #1 Presentation." In *The United Nations and the World's Religions: Prospects for a Global Ethic*, pp. 17–23. Cambridge, MA: Boston Research Center for the Twenty-First Century, 1995.

Fishbane, Michael. "The Image of the Human and the Rights of the Individual in Jewish Tradition." In *Human Rights and the World's Religions*, edited by Leroy S. Rouner, pp. 17–32. Notre Dame: University of Notre Dame Press, 1988.

Franck, Thomas M. *The Power of Legitimacy Among Nations*. New York: Oxford University Press, 1990.

Gandhi, Mohandas K. *An Autobiography: The Story of My Experiments With Truth*. Boston: Beacon Press, 1957.

Gendler, Rabbi Everett. "The Pursuit of Peace: A Singular Commandment." In *War and Its Discontents: Pacifism and Quietism in the Abrahamic Traditions*, edited by J. Patout Burns, pp. 31–46. Washington, DC: Georgetown University Press, 1996.

Gewirth, Alan. "The Golden Rule Rationalized." *Midwest Studies in Philosophy* 3 (1978): 133–47.

Goodman, Lenn E. "The Individual and the Community in the Normative Traditions of Judaism." In *Religious Diversity and Human Rights*, edited by Irene Bloom, J. Paul Martin, and Wayne L. Proudfoot, pp. 15–53. New York: Columbia University Press, 1996.

Goodman, Naomi. "Pacifism and Nonviolence: Another Jewish View." In *War and Its Discontents: Pacifism and Quietism in the Abrahamic Traditions*, edited by J. Patout Burns, pp. 67–73. Washington, DC: Georgetown University Press, 1996.

Gordis, Robert. "The Vision of Micah." In *Judaism and Human Rights*, edited by Milton R. Konvitz, pp. 278–87. New York: W. W. Norton, 1972.

Hall, David L., and Roger T. Ames. *Thinking Through Confucius*. Albany: State University of New York Press, 1987.

Hamidullah, Muḥammad. *Muslim Conduct of State*. Lahore: Sh. Muhammad Ashraf, 1987.

Harakas, Stanley S. "Human Rights: An Eastern Orthodox Perspective." In *Human Rights in Religious Traditions*, edited by Arlene Swidler, pp. 13–24. New York: Pilgrim Press, 1982.

Hashmi, Sohail H. "Is There an Islamic Ethic of Humanitarian Intervention?" *Ethics and International Affairs* 7 (1993): 55–73.

Hassan, Riffat. "On Human Rights and the Qur'anic Perspective." In *Human Rights in Religious Traditions*, edited by Arlene Swidler, pp. 51–65. New York: Pilgrim Press, 1982.

———. "Religious Human Rights and the Qur'an." *Emory International Law Review* 10 (1996): 85–96.

Hatcher, William S., and J. Douglas Martin. *The Bahá'í Faith: The Emerging Global Religion*. New ed. Wilmette, IL: Bahá'í Publishing, 2002.

Henkin, Louis. "Judaism and Human Rights." *Judaism* 25 (1976): 435–46.

Himes, Kenneth R. "Just War, Pacifism and Humanitarian Intervention." *America*, August 14, 1993, pp. 10–15, 28–31.

*The Holy Bible Containing the Old and New Testaments: New Revised Standard Version*. New York: Oxford University Press, 1989.

Hornby, Helen Bassett, comp. *Lights of Guidance: A Bahá'í Reference File*. 6th ed. New Delhi: Bahá'í Publishing Trust, 1999.

Huntington, Samuel P. *The Clash of Civilizations and the Remaking of World Order*. New York: Simon & Schuster, 1996.

Ishay, Micheline R. "Introduction." In *The Human Rights Reader: Major Political Writings, Essays, Speeches, and Documents From the Bible to the Present*, edited by Micheline R. Ishay, pp. xiii–xl. New York: Routledge, 1997.

Jayatilleke, K. N. "The Principles of International Law in Buddhist Doctrine." *Recueil des cours* 120 (1967): 441–567.

Johnston, Douglas. "Looking Ahead: Toward a New Paradigm." In *Religion, The Missing Dimension of Statecraft*, edited by Douglas Johnston and Cynthia Sampson, pp. 316–37. New York: Oxford University Press, 1994.

Jones, J. J., trans. *The Mahāvastu*. Vol. 1. London: Luzac, 1949.

Jordens, J. T. F. "Gandhi and the *Bhagavadgita*." In *Modern Indian Interpreters of the Bhagavadgita*, edited by Robert N. Minor, pp. 88–109. Albany: State University of New York Press, 1986.

Juergensmeyer, Mark. *The New Cold War? Religious Nationalism Confronts the Secular State*. Berkeley and Los Angeles: University of California Press, 1993.

Kelleher, Theresa. "Confucianism." In *Women in World Religions*, edited by Arvind Sharma, pp. 135–59. Albany: State University of New York Press, 1987.

Kellner, Menachem. "Jewish Ethics." In *A Companion to Ethics*, edited by Peter Singer, pp. 82–90. Oxford: Blackwell, 1993.

Khadduri, Majid. *War and Peace in the Law of Islam*. Baltimore: Johns Hopkins Press, 1955.

Kooijmans, P. H. "Protestantism and the Development of International Law." *Recueil des cours* 152 (1976): 81–117.

Küng, Hans. "Towards a World Ethic of World Religions." In *The Ethics of World Religions and Human Rights*, edited by Hans Küng and Jürgen Moltmann, pp. 102–19. London: SCM Press, 1990.

Küng, Hans, and Karl-Josef Kuschel, eds. *A Global Ethic: The Declaration of the Parliament of the World's Religions*. New York: Continuum, 1993.

Langan, John, S.J. "The Individual and the Collectivity in Christianity." In *Religious Diversity and Human Rights*, edited by Irene Bloom, J. Paul Martin, and Wayne L. Proudfoot, pp. 152–74. New York: Columbia University Press, 1996.

Legge, James, trans. *The Works of Menciusrm:*. Vol. 2 of *The Chinese Classics*. Hong Kong: Hong Kong University Press, 1960.

Lepard, Brian D. *Rethinking Humanitarian Intervention: A Fresh Legal Approach Based on Fundamental Ethical Principles in International Law and World Religions*. University Park: Pennsylvania State University Press, 2002.

Maimonides. "Treatise V: Laws Concerning Kings and Wars." In *The Code of Maimonides, Book Fourteen: The Book of Judges*, translated by Abraham M. Hershman, pp. 205–42. New Haven: Yale University Press, 1949.

———. "Treatise V: Laws Concerning Murder and the Preservation of Life." In *The Code of Maimonides, Book Eleven: The Book of Torts*, translated by Hyman Klein, pp. 193–236. New Haven: Yale University Press, 1954.

Marshall, Monty G., and Ted Robert Gurr et al. *Peace and Conflict 2005: A Global Survey of Armed Conflicts, Self-Determination Movements, and Democracy*. College Park: Center for International Development and Conflict Management, University of Maryland, 2005.

Mayer, Ann Elizabeth. *Islam and Human Rights: Tradition and Politics*. 3rd ed. Boulder: Westview Press, 1999.

McDonald, J. I. H. *Biblical Interpretation and Christian Ethics*. Cambridge: Cambridge University Press, 1993.

Mendelssohn, Moses. "Freedom of Religion—Absolute and Inalienable." In *Judaism and Human Rights*, edited by Milton R. Konvitz, pp. 179–89. New York: W. W. Norton, 1972.

Minor, Robert N. "The *Bhagavadgita* in Radhakrishnan's Apologetics." In *Modern Indian Interpreters of the Bhagavadgita*, edited by Robert N. Minor, pp. 147–72. Albany: State University of New York Press, 1986.

Nagler, Michael N. "Is There a Tradition of Nonviolence in Islam?" In *War and Its Discontents: Pacifism and Quietism in the Abrahamic Traditions*, edited by J. Patout Burns, pp. 161–66. Washington, DC: Georgetown University Press, 1996.

Nanda, Ved P. "International Law in Ancient Hindu India." In *Religion and International Law*, edited by Mark W. Janis and Carolyn Evans, pp. 51–61. The Hague: Martinus Nijhoff, 1999.

Niebuhr, Reinhold. "Optimism, Pessimism and Religious Faith—II." In Reinhold Niebuhr, *Christianity and Power Politics*, pp. 189–202. New York: Charles Scribner's Sons, 1940.

———. "Why the Christian Church Is Not Pacifist." In *The Essential Reinhold Niebuhr. Selected Essays and Addresses*, edited by Robert McAfee Brown, pp. 102–19. New Haven: Yale University Press, 1986.

Nussbaum, Arthur. *A Concise History of the Law of Nations*. New York: Macmillan, 1947.

Oppenheim, L. *International Law: A Treatise*. Vol. 1. New York: Longmans, Green, 1905.

Peters, Rudolph. *Jihad in Classical and Modern Islam: A Reader*. Princeton, N.J.: Markus Wiener, 1996.

Polish, Daniel F. "Judaism and Human Rights." In *Human Rights in Religious Traditions*, edited by Arlene Swidler, pp. 40–50. New York: Pilgrim Press, 1982.

Pollis, Adamantia. "Cultural Relativism Revisited: Through a State Prism." *Human Rights Quarterly* 18 (1996): 316–44.

Preston, Ronald. "Christian Ethics." In *A Companion to Ethics*, edited by Peter Singer, pp. 91–105. Oxford: Blackwell, 1993.

Rahman, Fazlur. *Major Themes of the Qur'ān*. Minneapolis: Bibliotheca Islamica, 1980.

Ramsey, Paul. *Basic Christian Ethics*. New York: Charles Scribner's Sons, 1953.

———. *The Just War: Force and Political Responsibility*. New York: Charles Scribner's Sons, 1968.

Rosenne, Shabtai. "The Influence of Judaism on the Development of International Law: A Preliminary Assessment." *Netherlands International Law Review* 5 (1958): 119–49.

Rost, H. T. D. *The Golden Rule: A Universal Ethic*. Oxford: George Ronald, 1986.

Ruether, Rosemary Radford. "Christianity." In *Women in World Religions*, edited by Arvind Sharma, pp. 207–33. Albany: State University of New York Press, 1987.

Sachedina, Abdulaziz A. "Freedom of Conscience and Religion in the Qur'an." In David Little, John Kelsay, and Abdulaziz A. Sachedina, *Human Rights and the Conflict of Cultures: Western and Islamic Perspectives on Religious Liberty*, pp. 53–90. Columbia: University of South Carolina Press, 1988.

———. "Justifications for Violence in Islam." In *War and Its Discontents: Pacifism and Quietism in the Abrahamic Traditions*, edited by J. Patout Burns, pp. 122–60. Washington, DC: Georgetown University Press, 1996.

al-Saleh, Osman Abd-el-Malek. "The Right of the Individual to Personal Security in Islam." In *The Islamic Criminal Justice System*, edited by M. Cherif Bassiouni, pp. 55–90. London: Oceana, 1982.

Salgado, Nirmala S. "Equality and Inequality in the Religious and Cultural Traditions of Hinduism and Buddhism." In *Equality and the Religious Traditions of Asia*, edited by R. Siriwardena, pp. 51–73. New York: St. Martins Press, 1987.

Sastry, K. R. R. "Hinduism and International Law." *Recueil des cours* 117 (1966): 503–615.

Schacht, Joseph. *An Introduction to Islamic Law*. Oxford: Clarendon Press, 1964.

Sharma, Arvind. *The Hindu Gītā: Ancient and Classical Interpretations of the Bhagavadgītā*. London: Duckworth, 1986.

————. "Hinduism." In *Our Religions*, edited by Arvind Sharma, pp. 1–67. New York: HarperCollins, 1993.

Sinaceur, Mohammed Allal. "Islamic Tradition and Human Rights." In Unesco, *Philosophical Foundations of Human Rights*, pp. 193–225. Paris: Unesco, 1986.

Smart, Ninian, and Richard D. Hecht, eds. *Sacred Texts of the World: A Universal Anthology*. New York: Crossroad, 1982.

Smith, Huston. *The World's Religions: Our Great Wisdom Traditions*. Rev. and updated ed. New York: HarperCollins, 1991.

Smith, Jane I. "Islam." In *Women in World Religions*, edited by Arvind Sharma, pp. 235–50. Albany: State University of New York Press, 1987.

*Tanakh: A New Translation of the Holy Scriptures According to the Traditional Hebrew Text*. Philadelphia: The Jewish Publication Society, 1985.

Thurman, Robert A. F. "Human Rights and Human Responsibilities: Buddhist Views on Individualism and Altruism." In *Religious Diversity and Human Rights*, edited by Irene Bloom, J. Paul Martin, and Wayne L. Proudfoot, pp. 87–113. New York: Columbia University Press, 1996.

Tutu, Desmond M. "Religious Human Rights and the Bible." *Emory International Law Review* 10 (1996): 63–68.

UN Millennium Project 2005. *Investing in Development: A Practical Plan to Achieve the Millennium Development Goals. Overview*. United Nations Development Program, 2005.

Unno, Taitetsu. "Personal Rights and Contemporary Buddhism." In *Human Rights and the World's Religions*, edited by Leroy S. Rouner, pp. 129–47. Notre Dame: University of Notre Dame Press, 1988.

Wattles, Jeffrey. *The Golden Rule*. New York: Oxford University Press, 1996.

Weeramantry, C. G. *Islamic Jurisprudence: An International Perspective*. New York: St. Martin's Press, 1988.

Wei-ming, Tu. "Confucianism." In *Our Religions*, edited by Arvind Sharma, pp. 139–227. New York: HarperCollins, 1993.

Weiming, Tu. "Epilogue: Human Rights as a Confucian Moral Discourse." In *Confucianism and Human Rights*, edited by Wm. Theodore de Bary and Tu Weiming, pp. 297–307. New York: Columbia University Press, 1998.

Wight, Martin. *International Theory: The Three Traditions*. Edited by Gabriele Wight and Brian Porter. New York: Holmes & Meier, 1992.

Wink, Walter. "Beyond Just War and Pacifism." In *War and Its Discontents: Pacifism and Quietism in the Abrahamic Traditions*, edited by J. Patout Burns, pp. 102–21. Washington, DC: Georgetown University Press, 1996.

Woodward, F. L., trans. *Some Sayings of the Buddha according to the Pali Canon*. London: Oxford University Press, 1973.

"Worldwide Adherents of All Religions by Six Continental Areas, Mid-2003." In "Religion," *2004 Encyclopaedia Britannica Book of the Year*, p. 280. Chicago: Encyclopaedia Britannica, 2004.

Yoder, John H. "On Not Being in Charge." In *War and Its Discontents: Pacifism and Quietism in the Abrahamic Traditions*, edited by J. Patout Burns, pp. 74–90. Washington, DC: Georgetown University Press, 1996.

Yoder, John Howard. *The Politics of Jesus: Vicit Agnus Noster.* 2nd ed. Grand Rapids, MI William B. Eerdmans Publishing, 1994.

Zaehner, R. C. *Hinduism.* London: Oxford University Press, 1966.

For more information about the Bahá'í Faith,
or to contact the Bahá'ís near you, visit
http://www.us.bahai.org/
or call
1-800-22-UNITE

*Bahá'í*
PUBLISHING
Wilmette, Illinois

# Bahá'í Publishing
## and the
# Bahá'í Faith

Bahá'í Publishing produces books based on the teachings of the Bahá'í Faith. Founded nearly 160 years ago, the Bahá'í Faith has spread to some 235 nations and territories and is now accepted by more than five million people. The word "Bahá'í" means "follower of Bahá'u'lláh." Bahá'u'lláh, the founder of the Bahá'í Faith, asserted that he is the Messenger of God for all of humanity in this day. The cornerstone of his teachings is the establishment of the spiritual unity of humankind, which will be achieved by personal transformation and the application of clearly identified spiritual principles. Bahá'ís also believe that there is but one religion and that all the Messengers of God—among them Abraham, Zoroaster, Moses, Krishna, Buddha, Jesus, and Muḥammad—have progressively revealed its nature. Together, the world's great religions are expressions of a single, unfolding divine plan. Human beings, not God's Messengers, are the source of religious divisions, prejudices, and hatreds.

The Bahá'í Faith is not a sect or denomination of another religion, nor is it a cult or a social movement. Rather, it is a globally recognized independent world religion founded on new books of scripture revealed by Bahá'u'lláh.

Bahá'í Publishing is an imprint of the National Spiritual Assembly of the Bahá'ís of the United States.

# Other Books Available from Bahá'í Publishing

## The Challenge of Bahá'u'lláh

by Gary L. Matthews

*Does God Still Speak to Humanity Today?*
Members of the Bahá'í Faith, the youngest of the independent world religions, represent one of the most culturally, geographically, and economically diverse groups of people on the planet, yet all are firmly united in their belief that the prophet and founder of their faith—Bahá'u'lláh (1817–1892), a Persian nobleman by birth—is none other than the "Promised One" prophesied in the scriptures of the world's great religions. Bahá'u'lláh Himself claimed to be the Messenger of God for humanity in this day, the bearer of a new revelation from God that will transform the human race.

Author Gary Matthews addresses the central question that anyone investigating the life, character, and writings of Bahá'u'lláh must ask: Is this remarkable figure really Who He claims to be? The author explains why he believes the revelation of Bahá'u'lláh is not only divine in origin, but also represents a unique challenge of unequaled importance to humanity today. Matthews sets forth the claims of Bahá'u'lláh, summarizes His teachings, and then embarks on his own examination. His investigation correlates Bahá'í prophecies with developments in history and science; considers Bahá'u'lláh's knowledge, wisdom, and character; describes His ability to reveal scripture and what it was like to be in His presence; discusses the profound influence of His writings; and more. Matthews concludes by inviting readers to make their own analysis of the record.
$15.00 / $18.00 CAN
ISBN 1-931847-16-9

# Close Connections: The Bridge between Spiritual and Physical Reality

by John S. Hatcher

Is consciousness a product of the soul or an illusion the brain creates? Has creation always existed, or does it have a point of beginning? Is matter infinitely refinable, or is there some indivisible building block for all of physical creation? Is the universe infinite or a finite "closed" system? Has the human being always been a distinct creation, or did we evolve from a lesser species? Is there a Creator whose design has guided the evolution of human society, or did creation and human society come about by pure chance? And if there is a Creator, why does He seem to allow injustice to thrive and the innocent to suffer so that we call natural disasters "acts of God"?

In *Close Connections* author and scholar John Hatcher employs axioms drawn from the Bahá'í Faith as tools for probing answers to these and other questions that relate to one overriding question: What is the purpose of physical reality? At the heart of the quest for these answers is a provocative analogy—a comparison of the creation and functioning of the individual human being with the method by which creation as a whole has come into being and progresses towards some as yet concealed destiny.

If the conclusions Hatcher draws from this study are correct, then every branch of science must in time reconsider its understanding of reality to include at least one additional dimension—the metaphysical or spiritual dimension—and its relationship to, and influence on, material reality.

$20.00 / $24.00 CAN
ISBN 1-931847-15-0

# Prophet's Daughter: The Life and Legacy of Bahíyyih Khánum, Outstanding Heroine of the Bahá'í Faith

by Janet A. Khan

The remarkable story of a woman who shaped the course of religious history. *Prophet's Daughter* examines the extraordinary life of Bahíyyih Khánum (1846–1932), the daughter of Bahá'u'lláh, founder of the Bahá'í Faith. During the mid-nineteenth and early twentieth centuries, when women in the Middle East were largely invisible, deprived of education, and without status in their communities, Bahíyyih Khánum was an active participant in the religion's turbulent early years and contributed significantly both to the development of its administrative structure and to its emergence as a worldwide faith community. Her appointment to head the Bahá'í Faith during a critical period of transition stands unique in religious history.

Bahíyyih Khánum's response to the events in her life despite some eight decades of extreme hardship illustrates her ability to transcend the social and cultural constraints of the traditional Muslim society in which she lived. Optimistic and resilient in the face of relentless persecution and uncertainty, practical and resourceful by nature, she embraced change, took action, and looked to the future. The legacy of her life offers an inspiring model for thoughtful women and men who seek creative ways to deal with social change and the pressures of contemporary life.

$18.00 / $22.00 CAN
ISBN 1-931847-14-2

# The Reality of Man

## Compiled by Terry J. Cassiday, Christopher J. Martin, and Bahhaj Taherzadeh

What Is a Human Being? What if it were possible for God to tell us why He created human beings? What if it were possible for Him to tell us the purpose of our existence?

Members of the Bahá'í Faith believe that just such information—and vastly more—is found in the revelation of Bahá'u'lláh, a body of work they consider to be the revealed Word of God. Bahá'u'lláh, Whose given name was Mírzá Ḥusayn-'Alí (1817–1892), was a Persian nobleman Who claimed to receive a new revelation from God fulfilling prophetic expectations of all the major religions while laying the foundation for a world civilization.

*The Reality of Man* presents a glimpse of the unique depth, range, and creative potency of Bahá'u'lláh's writings on such fundamental questions as What is a human being? What is the purpose of human existence? Where did we come from? Is there a God? What is God like? Do we each have a preordained role or mission in life? Is there life after death? Are some religions "true" and others "false"? How can one evaluate religions? Prepared by the editors at Bahá'í Publishing, this compilation also includes writings from Bahá'u'lláh's eldest son and designated successor, 'Abdu'l-Bahá (1844–1921), whose written works Bahá'ís

regard as authoritative.
ISBN 1-931847-17-7
$12.00 / $15.00 CAN

# The Story of Bahá'u'lláh:
# Promised One of All Religions

by Druzelle Cederquist

From the affluent courtyards of Tehran to the prison-city of Acre on the shores of the Mediterranean, *The Story of Bahá'u'lláh* brings to life in rich detail the compelling story of the prophet and founder of the Bahá'í Faith. Born to wealth and privilege, Bahá'u'lláh (1817–1892) was known as the "Father of the Poor" for His help to the needy. Yet despite His social standing, nothing could stop the forces that would have Him unjustly imprisoned in Tehran's notorious "Black Pit." Upon His release He was banished from Iran on a mountainous winter journey that His enemies hoped would kill Him.

Despite the schemes of His foes and the hardships of His exile, Bahá'u'lláh openly proclaimed the divine guidance revealed to Him. In over one hundred volumes, He delivered teachings on subjects ranging from the nobility of the soul to the prerequisites for the nations of the world to achieve a just and lasting peace.

The heart of His teaching was a new vision of the oneness of humanity and of the divine Messengers—among them Abraham, Moses, Buddha, Krishna, Christ, Muḥammad—Whom He claimed represent one "changeless Faith of God." Their teachings, He asserted, were the energizing force for the advancement of civilization. In 1863 Bahá'u'lláh announced He was the Messenger of God for humanity today and declared that His mission was to usher in the age of peace and prosperity prophesied in the scriptures of the world's great religions.

$15.00 / $18.00 CAN
ISBN 1-931847-13-4

To view our complete catalog, please visit
BahaiBooksUSA.com.